SOMETHING TO WRITE HOME ABOUT
Memories From a Presidential Diarist

© 2008 by Janis F. Kearney

All rights reserved. No part of this book may be reproduced or transmitted in any form or by any means, electronic or mechanical, including photocopying, recording or by any information storage and retrieval system, without permission in writing from Writing Our World Press, P.O. Box 164808, Little Rock, Arkansas 72216.

First Writing Our World Press Edition 2008
Printed in the United States of America

Edited by Mellonee Carrigan Mayfield
Book Design by Book Design Studio
Cover Design by Jennifer Tyson
Cover Photo by Jennifer Girard Photography

Library of Congress Control Number: 2008931711
ISBN: 9780976205852

www.writingourworldpress.com

For Sana'a and Darryl III

"Each day comes bearing its own gifts. Untie the Ribbons."
~ Ruth Ann Schabacker

SOMETHING TO WRITE HOME ABOUT

Memories From a Presidential Diarist

Janis F. Kearney

TABLE OF CONTENTS

		Page
Acknowledgements		vii
Introduction		ix
PART I	Ode to Varner Road (1953–1977)	1
PART II	Daisy and Me (1987–1992)	29
PART III	A Chapter in an Unfinished Life (1993)	63
PART IV	Something to Write Home About (1993–1995)	119
PART V	Almost Camelot (1996–1997)	177
PART VI	An American Presidency (1997–2000)	221
PHOTOS	Something to Write Home About: A Photo Journey	257
EPILOGUE	The Journey (January 20, 2001)	279
INTERVIEW	Q&A Session with Janis F. Kearney	301
INDEX		311

ACKNOWLEDGEMENTS

I'm neither smart enough, nor good enough to create a life as amazing as mine without divine guidance. Thus, I thank the higher power that traveled with me throughout my incredible journey. And though I've said it many times in many ways, I will forever be grateful to the man from Hope, Arkansas—William Jefferson Clinton, whose courage and belief in the American dream included someone like me.

As my parents taught me the real meaning of family by sheer example, by getting up each morning and demonstrating it, Bill Clinton showed me what great leadership looks like by doing it. By simply getting up each day believing that everyone deserves a shot at the American dream and by running a White House in a way to prove it. He taught me that it's not about perfection or pleasing everyone all the time.

Where would I be . . . who would I be had there been no James and Ethel Kearney? When I'm asked the question about heroes—and I'm forever being asked for some strange reason—James and Ethel Kearney are my initial responses every time.

There are so many other people who have had an impact on my life in important ways, including a few who made my time in the White House much richer. I am grateful to Nancy Hernreich, director of Oval Office Operations; Betty Currie, personal secretary to the president; the Oval Office Operations staff; and Bob Nash, director of Presidential Personnel, my closest friend and fellow life traveler.

And there was also Daisy Gatson Bates, who exhibited so much grace and courage, and who taught me the golden rule of making a difference no matter what your station in life.

Except for D.K., there would likely be no substantive journey to write about. His appearance in my life and his belief in me have always been the impetus for me to follow my dreams.

And finally, there is the Kearney clan, whose unconditional love and expectations helped shape and prepare me for the good and not so good in life. I can never thank my editor, Mellonee Carrigan Mayfield, whose many sleepless nights allow her to see beyond my words and make my story better. Also, special thanks to Marie Trotter and my book designer, Maria Karkucinski, for all the hard work on this book.

INTRODUCTION

"Troubles overcome are good to tell," says Canadian author Anne Marie McDonald, author of *The Way the Crow Flies*. Not only are they good, but they're also invaluable when it comes to the telling of my own personal troubles, which I choose to call *lessons learned*.

Growing up as one of James and Ethel Kearney's 19 children was key to these lessons as well as the journey from a cotton sharecropper's existence. It was an uneven and often troubled journey mixed with the best and worst of life, the harshest of realities and the most miraculous of possibilities.

Yet, journeys are about lessons; and even when it is most painful, there are abiding values. Thus, from the years I spent working Daddy's long cotton rows on Varner Road to that magical season I spent in a small corner office in the West Wing, each lesson was worth its weight in gold.

It would take me years to understand that it was those early sculptors of my life—my father, the dreamer, defined by his love for learning and teaching; and my mother, the beautiful stoic whose faith and love of family made bearable my harshest childhood realities—who prepared me for life's amazing journey.

Together, their examples transformed their children into shameless dreamers whose black-and-white realities kept those dreams grounded. The depth of disregard others had for this family of embarrassing numbers and providence propelled us dreamers to believe God heard our pitiful prayers or that he hid a special gift behind his back, waiting for the perfect time to present it.

We had to believe that God listened as intently to our small pleas as he did to the men who owned the land my father worked each year or to the one who drove a truck up to our door to deliver a copy of Daddy's loan papers with the word DENIED stamped across the front.

In spite of the harshest of my days, I offered those unwieldy dreams up to the seamless blue of the southeast Arkansas sky or sowed them in the long rows of green cotton stalks. And even during the achingly cold winters, the dreaming continued. Each handful of soft whiteness snatched from its boll was sprinkled with a different, grander, more ridiculous dream.

No one offered to tell me then, and thank God they didn't, that the dreams of a sharecropper's daughter weren't as likely to reach the heavens as those of a girl from the right side of the American dream, in the perfect home, protected by America's history that often assured her dreams would come true.

So I shake my head whenever I'm asked whether I dreamed that one day I'd meet a man who would one day become president or whether in a million years would I have dreamed of working inside the White House, and certainly never as the president's diarist.

That would have been a premonition. Dreams are neither guarantees, nor anything quite so specific. They are a process . . . the same as getting up to eat each day, or drinking water, or exercising on a regular basis. Your aim is to grow and be healthy, not necessarily that you will grow three inches rather than five. That just isn't the way dreams are.

Trusting that something absolutely miraculous can result from your dreams is the key. So is trusting enough to open your heart and soul to possibilities, to what can be.

There was always that knowledge subconsciously for much of my adult life that the dreams included a necessary spiritual or religious ingredient. It was believing that somebody up there, or somewhere, was looking out for me or understood how "impossible" these dreams were, but opted to do something about them anyway. With all that in place, our dreams very often make light of even our wildest expectations.

There were days, truthfully many days, that I stood as inconspicuously as possible—as inconspicuously as possible, given my dark skin and shoulder-length braids—pinching myself inside the White House complex or on the South Lawn. I often stood discreetly at the back of a crowd of political powerbrokers and rainmakers (mostly powerful white men, some women and a sprinkling of people who looked like me) all summoned together to celebrate some new law or to witness another lobby for change.

Though I rarely conversed with these distinguished guests, I believed some might also have been experiencing this out-of-body existence ... something beyond even their wildest dreams. Most wore gracious smiles; others, a look of expectancy ... and still others worked to exhibit the casualness of such an occasion.

We all listened, entranced, to William Jefferson Clinton's sonorous rasp and poetic cadence. Afterward there were whispers of fascination in the president's incredible ability to convince us all that life was as it should be or to urge us gently toward the realization that it was not.

In the midst of such days, I often daydreamed—much like those childhood years down on Varner Road, out in Daddy's cotton field. I was often struck by the convergence of our destinies: that America's 42nd president, who beat the odds in spite of his Arkansas roots, and a daughter of Arkansas sharecroppers should in different ways become ripples of change in American and presidential history.

It was a time of deep pride in being American and in a presidency held by many in admiration and awe. Some compared the era to that of John F. Kennedy's Camelot. The world would later question America's wisdom in shining a blinding light on our leader's weaknesses.

On those days, however, hundreds of men and women, CEOs and leaders from every corner, every walk of life were enraptured by this leader as he gently jerked our heartstrings or pealed a bell in our souls.

There was an otherworldliness to those days, and I'd have to remind myself not to wallow in the magic, that God didn't make stardust permanent. I would talk to myself as I sat unobtrusively at the back of the room during some important meeting, reminding myself that my being there in the middle of Earth-shaking decisions only made God yawn.

One reporter likened my job during the Clinton years to that of a fly on the wall of the Clinton White House. I've always liked that analogy. For sure, I wasn't there to make or advise on policies or laws. I wasn't a politician in the true sense of the word, though I'd been greatly entertained by my father's rants about politicians as a child.

Politics. Oh, how I'd fought against it. I hated the whole idea of trying to please all the people all the time merely for their vote. But I learned that my view had been narrow after all. Politics is as much a part of the American dream as the American campaigns and elections. It is intrinsic to our lives no matter how much we claim differently.

Watching a young Bill Clinton use politics for 12 years to help change the face of Arkansas government helped to steer me in that final decision.

I was invited into the Clinton White House in 1995 as a silent observer to document the ripples of change in American and presidential history. In fact, it was the intended invisibility of my role that drew me there—a shadow shadowing a president and chronicling his days, becoming familiar with the American presidency from firsthand observation. My past allowed me to observe the president's days through an outsider's eyes rather than as a White House insider.

Was I able to be objective? That is one of those questions I always expect when I speak to an audience about those days. Who is ever completely objective about anything in our lives?

Our views begin their evolutions the day we are brought into this world and are colored by so many things outside our power long before we realize we have opinions at all.

In that role, in any role, we bring our pasts, our likes, our jealousies, our prejudices into every decision we make. Ask any of the most celebrated judges to be honest about this, and my guess is if they're honest, they'll tell you this is true.

Was there a conflict given my unadulterated awe of the place, the process, and, yes, the person I was there to observe and document? Yes, an unadulterated "Yes!" I fell in love with American and presidential history during those days inside the White House.

It was a thrill to watch a president do presidential things—interact with celebrated visitors or his brilliant aides, or trade niceties with the very old or young congressmen who'd painted the ugliest picture of him earlier in the day.

All these men (and a handful of women) had one thing in common—that aura of power, that same power that set George Washington and Thomas Jefferson apart from the rest of the world.

It was awe-inspiring to see this side of the American dream, this American president up close in the flesh changing America in great and lasting ways, yet falling short in other less important ways.

More than anything, I knew that politics wasn't just for the rich or the powerful, but that with the right person at the helm and if given half a chance, it really could work for all America. And we almost made it.

What a wonderful class in American government those five years turned out to be. What an amazing journey! I was reminded more than once during that time of my first titillating brush with political science. Who was it that named politics a science, rather than an art . . . a skill of human relationships?

My only class in political science was in the early '70s at the very same university that Bill Clinton and Hillary Rodham taught law to three of my seven brothers who became lawyers. It was around that time that I sat in the late Diane Blair's American History class at the University of Arkansas and fell in love with the theory of good government. God, did that woman have the gift of making you feel that America and the White House belonged to everyone!

But, like most Americans, I had only a vague and distant familiarity with the presidency and the White House before 1993. I'd watched and listened as presidents delivered their State of the Union addresses. My interest was piqued along with others' during campaign seasons as the candidates made their promises and criticized their opponents.

My father, who turned 102 in 2008, had his own brush with the presidency when, as a young vagabond in the 1920s, he'd jumped off the train in the nation's capital and happened upon 16th and Pennsylvania. An avid reader and lover of history even then, he'd stood peering through the White House gates, hoping to get a look at then-President Warren G. Harding.

"I never expected to see any black man working inside that place," James Kearney would tell his children years later.

The thought that never traveled too far from my mind as I walked those hallowed grounds was that it had been home to 40 American presidents. Each, except George Washington, had called this place home. I'd studied most of these men, and my early studies had taught me they were almost on par with God. These fallacies contributed to the awe most of us felt about our presidents and the White House.

My adult studies told me just how far most of these men were from God and just how pitifully few in this group would have imagined someone like me inside those hallowed halls. These were mostly good men whose imperfections included inherent prejudices and preconceived perceptions of others based on something as shallow as the color of one's skin.

My role in the White House was more than a miracle for someone with my pedigree—or lack of it. I was a part of a new era in the American presidency, one ushered in by a young Southern governor from a small town called Hope, in a small state known more for its negatives than anything good or memorable.

Those not born of poverty or of a group America has dubbed the "oppressed" might not imagine what I felt as I walked or rode through the northwest gates into the White House each morning; as I stood inside the Oval Office and spied the South Lawn awakened by the sun, the dew still glistening on the perfectly manicured grass, or the Rose Garden with its sea of color. Those mornings were times of intermingling emotions—memories of

Introduction

my yesterdays and continuing awe that my journey had deposited me at the White House, so far from where I'd begun.

So many of my parents' teachings invaded my thoughts during those years, about how each man must be rated based on his contributions, not his mistakes; and that it is only other men who remember our errors, while God takes note of our deeds.

Finally, and most gratefully, I would never forget the one most important lesson from Varner Road: that when we believe in our dreams, in those most inconceivable of possibilities, we open the door to a reality that's loftier than all of our dreams.

PART I

ODE TO VARNER ROAD

(1953–1977)

I could never write about such a critical chapter in my life without reflecting on what is still the most important time in my life—my time on Varner Road. By the time 1993 rolled around, Varner Road had changed a great deal from what it was during my childhood. But much on that eight-mile stretch remained as it was during the 17 years I called it home.

The road was still caked with gravel for better transport of the farmers' heavy machinery. It was still enshrined by overgrown trees and cotton and soybean fields worked by white farmers and black inmates from Cummins Prison.

On my weekly visits to Varner Road, I still often came upon a field of black men in dizzying white uniforms with their backs bent forward as they yanked their hoes to remove patches of grass from among the beautiful green vegetables growing on the prison's farm. These men worked silently while a smaller group of white men sat tall atop horses, cradling large guns. Some things, it seems, would never change on Varner Road.

In spite of America's and Arkansas' trudge forward, Varner Road still held claim on me as sure as the DNA that ran in my blood. There was Varner Road, and there were James and Ethel Kearney. And the three represented everything good and important and life sustaining about that place and time.

Varner Road is how I measure my journey, how I view my victories and failures, my distances stretched out behind me or that which is yet left to travel. It is a constant reminder of why I cannot claim my journey as simply mine.

It was on Varner Road, thanks to the starkness of life I experienced there, that I learned to view people and life events in something more than black and white. It is because of the miracles of that phase of my life that blessings are never taken for granted.

It is there along those eight miles of gravel and in those woods that I came to understand the burden of others' prejudgments and vowed to try and live my life without the taint of blindly prejudging another human being. And thanks to that time, I learned to look beyond what is in front of me, what my eyes allow, to search for what is in the heart.

There has never been a sliver of hope that I would make an effective criminal prosecutor or a successful, strict disciplinarian. I have the knotty problem of searching for the root causes of others' actions, others' existence.

Scientists, I am told, have proclaimed that most human beings are pretty much "set in stone" by the time they are 4 years old. I am amazed and troubled by this. What of all the children born to parents who don't have the emotional or material wherewithal to raise them up right? Are they simply a lost cause?

What about the millions of adults who spend decades trying to change who they are to become better human beings, to create a better future? Are they, too, wasting their time and effort, their dreams and fervent prayers?

Most of us accept science at face value. And while this edict is hard to swallow, I assume scientists know from which they speak. Yet, what of those miracles I was taught to believe in down on Varner Road . . . the miracle of dreams and hopes and prayers? Where would I be . . . no, where would the 17 Kearney children, who grew up on Varner Road, be were there no such thing as miracles? Had we simply accepted that our fate was written in stone during our toddler years? Had we given up and let reality take its course?

Varner Road presented my siblings and me with the dubious, but very real gift of living without, but knowing that tomorrow held the promise of something different, something more. That insatiable hunger that comes from having so little and wanting so much evolved into the Kearney trait of dreaming and hoping and believing in a better tomorrow.

Others' perception of our nothingness taught us to honor our own sense of what is important in life and to eschew others' values. We were rich in so many ways that others couldn't fathom.

Varner Road gave us the deep sense of family that remains to this day. We can dislike each other so much we don't want to hear that particular sibling's voice one day, then the very next day forget the reason for the silly squabble and spend hours laughing with each other.

Our parents, thankfully, drilled the importance of family into us—showing us the importance of independence when it came to the world but interdependence on each other. And oftentimes that meant loving each other, even those times when we didn't like each other.

This was one of the seeds they planted that allowed us to never feel alone in the world or to be without a best friend when others shunned us. Our familial love was deepened, I'm convinced, by our familiarity with having so little. That shared knowledge evolved over time into our collective hunger for more than we saw and experienced on Varner Road.

———

Though we certainly didn't see it during our formative years, we would later realize what wise parents James and Ethel really were. They never said, "Nothing is free from question . . . never be satisfied with the pat answers to life."

Yet, it was that unspoken understanding that we were to forge our own way and use our brains and our hearts to decide how to take care of ourselves and be most useful to the world. And, of course, they would never say that religion was just a part of life; that there is also living and the world—and we have to give each its due priority.

My father was a dreamer, a self-taught intellect, and a tilter of windmills. My mother, maybe a dreamer as well, was more than anything a pragmatist who showed us grace in the face of life's stresses. She exhibited self-discipline and perseverance. Together, these two under-educated parents—whose lives revolved around working their cotton crops, having babies every 12 or 18 months and raising us up to be responsible citizens of the world—taught us that hopes and dreams are antithesis to accepting things as they are.

Varner Road was, indeed, a village where not only everyone knew everyone, but also where only the most private of secrets remained secrets. We knew our neighbor's fears, their weaknesses, their losses and victories.

While it may be true that nothing times nothing equals nothing, it is also true that when members of a village share what little they have with the rest of the village, survival is guaranteed for all.

We survived as a family because of James and Ethel Kearney. We survived as a village because neighbors believed we all somehow belonged to each other, took responsibility for each other. Other families on Varner Road helped prop us up, filled in the crevices and closed the gaps left by the harshness of our existence.

How many times did one of us run barefoot down Varner Road or across the soybean field to a neighbor's home to borrow a cup of sugar, a bag of flour, eggs or flavoring for a Sunday church function?

The neighbor would fill the cup or pour flour in a bag or place the eggs in a box and go back to her household chores. She might holler out the door as we left, "You be careful going back across that field . . . Don't you drop them eggs."

There was never the question of why parents didn't have their own. Tomorrow or the next day, it might be their youngster running to our home or the house down the road to borrow what they didn't have.

As an adult I've learned a great deal about the humanness of those adults I saw as "old" or "backward" or "illiterate." They might have been all those things, but their hearts made them giants. Good, but very human, giants.

The sins of saints, I learned, are as common as the sins of avowed sinners. Oh, the things I later learned about the goings-on down on Varner Road. The romantic dalliances, the jealousies, the children born out of wedlock ... transgressions I would never, as a child, have attached to the grown-ups on Varner Road.

And while those truths about the people on Varner Road left me a little surprised or a bit disillusioned, they did not make me love or revere those good people any less. None of these later discoveries overshadowed the important roles they played in my life.

―

There was always a hint of nostalgia in my father's voice when he talked about the large number of families that lived on Varner Road when he and my mother moved there in the early '40s. They had lived in a number of places, all in the general area of Jefferson and Lincoln counties, before settling on a small piece of land belonging to the black Wilkins family of Pine Bluff. They described them fondly as a wealthy Negro family.

When I was born, my parents didn't live immediately on Varner Road, but about a mile off the gravel road. That home sat in the middle of a few acres of land and was surrounded by a wonderful fruit orchard. As a young girl, I recall the giant trees and the smell of fresh apples, peaches and pears in the summer.

I also remember the pecan tree that sat up the hill from the soybean field between our home and the home of Robert and Nola Mae Jackson. We were never sure who exactly owned it, but we regularly robbed that poor tree of its pecans.

It was on the Wilkins farm that I first sat in Daddy's lap and steered a tractor as he drove across the fields. I ran home later and told all my siblings that I could drive Daddy's John Deere tractor. A few years later, I would, in fact, drive it for a few minutes at least on my own.

I grew up during the innocent '50s, a time when my family fell asleep at night without the slightest fear that anyone would invade our privacy or harm us. There were no locks on our doors, ever. Many times, during those pleasantly cool summer nights our doors remained open all night. In summer, the windows were never closed except when it rained.

Varner Road was a community. Families and homes were strewn up and down the gravel road. It wouldn't be until the '60s that individuals, then families, began moving away en masse. Back then, there was no official name for the slow, but consistent departures.

Decades later, though, intellectuals, and historians would define it as The Great Migration. Obviously, this unusually high number of blacks leaving the South for better opportunities in the North and Midwest deserved studying, and an official name.

Years later, when I began to travel through the states, I met elderly men and women who remembered my parents and Varner Road with a mixture of fondness and nostalgia. They would tell me how they had no option, except to leave.

"We left so that we could live," I'd hear over and over again. An incredible number of these migrants, now living in Chicago, California, New York or Detroit, had lived within or near our community. Some had attended

Rankin Chapel Church where Daddy, much younger then, was the Sunday school superintendent.

Like so many others from regions dependent on a disappearing agricultural economy, their families also had sought something more than the cotton fields and the meager wages of cotton labor.

Even as the population declined, Varner Road remained a village, a community of families who all knew each other and who all helped each other when they could. So many people in their small and large ways had an impact on my family's lives and mine.

Some, like us, lived directly adjacent to Varner Road with nothing separating us but a sizable front yard that was home to chickens, geese, guinea and less-than-useful dogs. Others who claimed a Varner Road address lived truly "in the country," but still near enough to the gravel road to walk the few miles to catch a ride to town or to visit.

It was a mixed community of black, white and, over time, a few brown families. The few Mexican migrant workers from way across the Texas border had somehow found their way into our part of the world. They came in search of seasonal work, to put down temporary roots or, if they were lucky, to secure permanent work. These workers and their families added to the richness of our small world.

Every man, and most women, on Varner Road spent most of their waking hours working by the sweat of their brow. Farming sustained all of us. A farmer's distinction was measured by the size of his farming equipment.

White farmers who grew hundreds of acres of cotton and soybeans—and later wheat and rice—had machinery that forced cars to move off the road into the ditch as they drove by.

Some black farmers, like our neighbors the Calloways, were large farmers, as well—large enough to need to hire day laborers to help "the Calloway boys" plow and rotate their crops. They also hired field hands who chopped the cotton in the spring and summer and picked the cotton in the fall.

Some summers, to our embarrassment, my siblings and I were a part of our next-door neighbors' hired day workers. Social scientists would likely find it interesting that black day laborers found it more humiliating to work in each other's fields than to work in the white farmer's fields. This showed friends and neighbors just how far down the economic and social totem pole we really were.

Sharecropping, we would later learn, was a common farming relationship between former slaves and white landowners in Arkansas as well as in many other Southern states. James Kearney, though, was the only black farmer we knew who still called himself a sharecropper into the late '60s; and it was hardly something that made us proud.

We often wondered if there was another father, like James Kearney, whose 50 acres were borrowed or leased; or if there were other families of 17 children whose livelihoods depended on the success of their crops each year. What an inordinate amount of hope and dependence we placed on Mother Nature.

My brothers helped out with many of the harsher chores of farming—clearing and rotating the fields between seasons; plowing the fields to prepare them for planting; then working along with the rest of us who chopped the grass and weeds from the cotton fields during the spring and summer.

We all took part in that summer chore of chopping cotton and the more reviled winter task of picking cotton from the age of 7 until we left home for college.

Daddy had the basic necessities in farming equipment to work his land. Some of my older siblings often talked about "Old Bessie," the mule, who helped them maintain the crops for years before Daddy bought the John Deere tractor on credit.

Though he would eventually raise soybeans, Daddy never raised enough to require his owning a combine—the machine that threshed and harvested the soybean seeds once they were ripened. My father would hire a worker on a larger farm to harvest the soybeans.

By the late '60s, it was evident that agriculture was changing right before our eyes and that manual labor, and certainly work that involved farm crops, would not remain a viable option for many Southern blacks whose livelihoods had for decades depended on farming.

Though my siblings and I were still being hired out to large, white farmers during the latter half of our summer "vacations," there was a steadily growing number of farmers in the area who no longer used field hands or laborers to remove grass and weeds from their cotton fields. There were already miles of cotton fields never touched by a hoe or human hand.

Gratefully, most of the Kearney children had graduated from high school by the time these changes were universal and permanent in the South. How in the world would we have gotten by had that not been the case? We depended exclusively on those last six weeks of the summer to earn money for our school clothing and supplies, and to help our family out.

Daddy never seriously considered moving away "up North" like many other black families chose to do. I've often wondered how our lives would have differed, how we would have been different people had our parents acquiesced to suggestions to move to "the city".

I simply can't imagine it. Daddy had worked many jobs and in just about every region of the country during his young life. That, however, was before he returned to southeast Arkansas at age 26—something of a prodigal son—and met and fell instantly in love with 19-year-old Ethel Virginia Curry. They would marry three months later and raise 17 of their 19 children down on Varner Road.

I have often wondered if our two oldest siblings who grew up with their other parents and in other environments were spared or missed out by not growing up as we did.

I could never get my imagination around the picture of Daddy working in a car factory or steel mill until he was 62 years old . . . or Mama staying home and raising 17 urban kids; being forced to learn to drive; being boxed into a small, three-bedroom subsidized apartment.

I could no more imagine the young Kearney clan walking a few blocks each day to an urban school with either its urban problems or its urban benefits. I did, however, sometimes dream of living in a place where I could walk into a public library as often as I wanted and check out as many books as I wanted!

But lots of black families did choose the option of leaving the South. The slow but steady trek of black families from Varner Road to the promise of a better life in Midwestern and Northern cities continued for more than 20 years.

By the time I left in 1971, there were roughly 20 families still living up and down Varner Road. This was a far cry from the 100 or so families that had lived there during my earliest years.

This transformation then was just about economics. There were upheavals in the status quo all across the country. The racial conflicts that had dogged America for so long were evident right there in Gould, Arkansas, and were an impetus for so much that changed during that time.

Blacks who had been satisfied and grateful for the menial farm jobs and the constant end-of-the-month pay were now becoming discontent with the inequities involved in manual labor.

At the same time, large farmers—almost all of them white—were seeking ways to make raising cotton more profitable, thus cutting out the need for the now disgruntled manual laborer. In the larger arena of agriculture, cotton was no longer king in rural America. It was becoming too expensive to be profitable.

In spite of social scientists' decree about black families, most homes on Varner Road were headed by two parents. There were some instances of grandparents being the sole caretakers. Daughters or sons who had moved away to the cities to find jobs often found it too difficult to make ends meet with a child.

Some parents who moved North sent their children to "the country" for summer vacations, but due to personal hardships opted to make the South a permanent home for their child. Even while the South still wrestled with racial inequities, there was something to be said for the basic quality of life for children who grew up in the country.

There were three churches on Varner Road during that time: Rankin Chapel, First Baptist and Dora Bell—all three were black churches. I'm not sure where the white residents attended church. Almost half of the black families attended Rankin Chapel, while the other half attended First Baptist. Most of the members of Dora Bell lived eight miles north of Gould in the small town of Grady.

Varner Road had its share of transient families, not just the migrant families who followed the seasons, but small families who rented or homesteaded for a few months or a year, then decided to move on.

During my years on Varner Road, there were several Mexican families, all migrant farmers, who lived in the community. I became bus friends with the daughter of one migrant family when I attended Gould Junior High School.

Frances was enrolled in the school for one full spring semester. Like me, she was a quiet, but friendly girl, and we would often sit together during the bus ride to school and sometimes on the way home.

I was surprised to learn that Frances spoke fluent English. I learned a lot about the migrant culture from that brief friendship. Even while I was in awe of their moving around so often, I knew it wasn't a life I could ever get used to.

As exciting as my father's stories were about his early vagabond life, I had always needed a home, and I worried that Frances and other migrant children never knew for sure where they might lay their heads at night.

⌒

Politics wasn't a word commonly used by my parents or other adults down on Varner Road. When Daddy had something good or bad to say about the new laws or congressional bills that would have an impact on our lives, he'd say, "The damn government is at it again." He rarely referred to any specific person or leader. It was the whole kit and caboodle—the government.

Sometimes, the strange sounds that came from Daddy's throat didn't always mean he wanted to tie up a bunch of those politicians in a croker sack and pitch them out in the bayou. Sometimes, it simply meant, "It's about time somebody up there finally got it right."

For Daddy, most politicians represented the heartless government—be it the president, governor or some congressman in Washington.

Oh, the poor presidents. The little I do remember about the presidents from my early years was how they unknowingly received the brunt of Daddy's vitriolic ranting. He would let us know when these lawmakers had either messed up a perfectly good law that should have changed things for the better or had stood lamely by while the narrow-minded leaders in Arkansas allowed things to get worse.

Ode to Varner Road (1953–1977)

There weren't many "attaboys" directed at the government or political leaders when I was growing up on Varner Road.

James Kearney didn't deal in grays when it came to politics or the Good Book. You either lived by the law of the Good Book, or you broke that law. The political leaders were either on our side, or they weren't. Ironically, while a liberal politician was OK in Daddy's book, a liberal Christian had likely paved his road straight to hell.

Daddy blamed the Vietnam War on both John F. Kennedy and Lyndon B. Johnson. The war was one of the few shared responsibilities of two different presidents. Although these were two of his favorite presidents, they often drew Daddy's wrath for making the stupid decision to send our boys over to meddle in another country's affairs.

Daddy always had a thing about America meddling in another country's affairs, especially when it failed so miserably in straightening out some basic things here in our own country. "Who gave us the right? God?" he'd ask.

It wasn't just a matter of a conflict where innocent young men were dying in somebody else's war, it was the gall of America to always think it knew how to run another country the right way, Daddy would argue. "Look at the mess we're in over here!" he'd say to no one in particular. We weren't allowed to respond, and Mama usually chose not to.

LBJ got Daddy's admiration for his strong, albeit slow, response to the civil rights demands. He also got kudos for making racial integration a federal law. As happy as Daddy was that the government finally made integration a law, he was never one of those who believed it would be the answer to all our problems.

My parents, like most Americans—both blacks and whites—were swept up into the Camelot era of the Kennedy administration. They thought John Kennedy was a good president, though Daddy worried that Kennedy's wealth might be a detriment to his understanding the needs of poor, black folks. But Daddy did admit the young, handsome president made people proud to be Americans.

Kennedy was the first president I actually paid any real attention to when he spoke on television. I was 7 when he was elected in 1960, and I vividly remember his assassination in 1963. But his transformational presidency and his death were springboards to my interest in American presidents.

Daddy, like most blacks—make that most Americans—thought Franklin D. Roosevelt was the greatest president in our history. Not even Abraham Lincoln, who (some say begrudgingly) freed the slaves, was held in such high esteem.

Yet, as much as Daddy revered Roosevelt, he believed FDR was too timid when it came to America's race problem. He helped us by default, Daddy said. He believed Roosevelt wrapped his whole presidency around World War II and, because of that, ignored the race problems going on right under his nose.

By the time I was 10 years old, I could identify our governors pretty well. I guess I have Governor Orval Faubus to thank for that when his stand against the integration of Little Rock's Central High School made him an international figure. Then, of course, there were the

Ode to Varner Road (1953–1977)

highly volatile gubernatorial campaigns, like the year the far, far right conservative and avowed Ku Klux Klan proponent Jim Johnson proved how a politician's negatives assured him a place in history.

Winthrop Rockefeller, of course, was one of Arkansas' most colorful governors and the first Republican to temporarily lure Daddy to cross party lines in 1964 for the first time in his voting history.

Some Republicans swore Rockefeller was Republican in name only, and that suited Daddy just fine. Daddy didn't mind, either, that others said Rockefeller bought the governor's mansion. He believed they all did one way or another.

Though there is much to remember about Rockefeller's colorful personal life, his tenure as governor included taking some serious stabs at changing the complexion of an all-white state government. He would lay a foundation that the next three Arkansas governors—all Democrats—would build on.

Immediately following Rockefeller's governorship came smart, moderate Democrat Dale Bumpers. He was followed by Governor David Pryor. These two men were well regarded by most Arkansans, and both were credited with moving Arkansas toward the 20th century. For that, they were awarded national roles in the U.S. Senate, roles that were theirs until they chose to retire after more than 30 years of service.

Arkansas' youngest and most popular governor, William Jefferson Clinton, followed David Pryor. He had served as the state's attorney general and, directly from that role, began campaigning for the senior role in the state.

Bill Clinton was elected governor in 1978, and my father immediately took to this young man, who talked his kind of talk—attempting to level the playing field, reforming the education system, and taking care of the poor and elderly.

When Bill Clinton spoke, my parents sat smiling and nodding at the television. While Daddy had been pleased with Governor Bumpers and Governor Pryor, he saw in Clinton the possibility of a governor who could change things in a more structural way.

I was an adult, no longer living at home on Varner Road, when I was actually allowed to discuss politics with my father. I was amazed at his political intelligence and his realization of the important role politics played in our lives—never mind the fact that he bad-mouthed such a large number of politicians.

While many poor and not-so-poor blacks in Lincoln County eschewed voting or getting involved in politics, saying their votes wouldn't make a difference, Daddy never took that position.

Even with his frequent cynical rants about government leaders, James Kearney understood that black folks' quest for change demanded that we play a part in that change. And the simplest way to do it was by getting out and voting. He saw our participation in politics as a basic responsibility, just as equality, freedom and job opportunities should be every citizen's right.

We didn't call it politics down on Varner Road, but later I would know that what we experienced in Gould was unadulterated politics. Most memorable of that time was

In fact, our family had nothing to be ashamed of. We didn't lie in wait for a check each month. We were a hardworking family, little different from most families I knew. Where, I often wondered, did the myth of the lazy black man or woman grow roots? Certainly, not from observing the men, women and families on Varner Road—all proud Americans who believed that an honest day's work was synonymous with pleasing God . . . and pleasing God was important in our communities.

The failure of the welfare system wasn't the fault of people like those who lived on Varner Road. More than anything else, it was the fault of a federal government that refused to intervene in the poorest of our citizens' lives in the areas where we needed it most—jobs, education and health care.

Daddy's drives to the "government office" in the nearby town of Star City in his 1953 Chevy pickup truck are memorable because his return included several big boxes of welfare food.

The sturdy cardboard boxes held thick blocks of yellow cheese; butter that had a rich aroma that burst through its wrapper; shiny, silver cans of chopped pork or chopped beef; heavy, thick peanut butter; or split peas—the only green vegetable I refused to eat during my childhood. The boxes of food were the epitome of the Kearney family's love-hate relationship with the government.

Daddy would have preferred a small loan to purchase his own piece of land, rather than continue to rent another man's land and resort to welfare food to get through the winters. "If they'd given us the 40 acres, we wouldn't need their welfare," he'd complain.

Yet, the handouts often helped us make it through the winters when Daddy's cotton crops failed us. "Welfare winters," Daddy would later call them. Pride was one thing, and he had plenty of it, but feeding his family was more important to him than his pride.

James Kearney never bit his tongue as he ranted about the man-made laws that benefited the rich and punished the poor. His best example of the worst form of government was in the shape of the agriculture extension agent who drove up into our yard, blowing his horn for Daddy to come out to discuss some matter of business. We could see Daddy's face and body harden when the man drove up and even after he'd left.

Over the years, the extension agent's visits would transform Daddy from an easy-going, jovial father, who loved spending his evenings telling us stories, to an angry sharecropper who blasted the racist system that refused him the breaks he deserved.

Toiling the 50 acres he and Mama leased for their cotton crops was how Daddy released his resentment against the government and his bitterness at the "system."

Even then, politics played a role in our lives. Many of the black folks in Gould and on Varner Road listened intently as Daddy talked about the importance of voting and even who he thought the best man for the job was.

He took this constitutional right very seriously, going as far as hauling truckloads of friends and strangers to the polls on Election Day. Daddy would spend part of the night cursing the "damn poll taxes—another way for the white man to hold us down."

In spite of his bitterness at the South's political and social system, James Kearney was the first to point out that there were good white folks just as there were bad Negroes.

My parents' wall of heroes tacked above their poster bed included pictures of President Kennedy, Robert Kennedy, Martin Luther King Jr., and Daisy Bates. These people in the photos, which came from the Dollar Store or the *Pine Bluff Commercial* newspaper, were the ones my parents believed had an impact on our lives and changed our world for the better.

Most Americans over 50 recall that exciting, but frightening, experimental time in America when the names Kennedy and King meant change—not just for blacks or whites, but for America. These two men represented change in a country that revered tradition and the past.

The town leaders in places like Gould would have described those times as dangerous for their towns and for America. Many resented how much of their time was being diverted to the new civil rights laws. They were all afraid of what these changes would mean for their town and their people.

As a child, I wouldn't have recognized that politics and these two young leaders' ideals had anything to do with the fact that we rode buses that sometimes broke down before they arrived at our school or that there were bathrooms meant to serve hundreds of students that were left unrepaired for weeks at a time or windows that were left broken for a full school term.

I was too young to question why some of my friends who lived near the white school, which had a lot more rooms and space for children than ours did, never chose to attend that school ... or why buses carrying white children to their school couldn't simply stop and pick us up and drop us off at our school.

How long did I enjoy the "secondhand" books passed on to me from the white school before someone told me that the books somehow painted me as "secondhand"? Had I not been told, I would have thought our teachers purchased the books at the same secondhand store in Pine Bluff where my parents shopped.

As young children, we didn't know there was a negative connotation to something being secondhand. It was the only way my parents could clothe their houseful of children. And for us, it was simply part of our lives—nothing to feel ashamed about. Whether it was from Saks or M.M. Cohn or secondhand, at that time, we didn't know the difference.

School was a blessing, a godsend, as far as we were concerned. It meant free books, an opportunity to sit in class and learn something I didn't know the day before, to read stories sometimes out loud, to lose myself in stories of Dick and Jane, and Sally and Spot.

I learned early on that, as shy as I've always been, reading out loud was the easiest thing in the world for me. I suddenly became someone else, an extension of myself, not little Janis Faye Kearney. To me, that was the magic of books and reading.

When the teacher handed us our books for the school year in September, it was as if she was handing me a sliver of gold. Daddy had taught us that reverence for books, and I'd fawn over mine as if they were, indeed, something I could exchange for valuables. I had no idea (I wonder now if I would have cared) that a white child owned that very book when it was brand new and that it was only after the white students had used it up (like chewing the sweetness from gum) that it was shipped over to the black school. Did that mean we were second-hand people?

Learning from hand-me-down books, however, didn't dampen my excitement about learning. It didn't matter that Lisa or Diane or Cecelia's names were already written in swooping curlicues inside the front cover in the space marked: This Book Belongs To.

Did it mean, though, that other children had learned the good things inside that book a lot earlier than we would, and now we'd always be running to catch up? Even their learning it first hadn't negated my opportunity for learning it, too, albeit secondhand.

Yes, my childhood on Varner Road was infiltrated with outcomes, decisions, policies that had trickled down from our state and federal politicians. Politics was a part of our lives even when it was the farthest thing from our minds. Because of politics, the Kearneys and others in Gould would be fraught with challenges and hardships. These, I later learned, were opportunities to learn lessons that I could tuck away for later use.

PART II

DAISY AND ME

(1987–1992)

Two life-changing events took place in August 1987: the death of my sister Jo Ann, at the age of 32, after more than a decade of suffering from mental illness; and my re-acquaintance with Arkansas' own civil rights legend, Daisy Gatson Bates, 16 years after our first brief meeting.

Mrs. Bates was someone I'd long admired. And during the summer of my junior year in high school, she was someone I dreamed of working for.

In the mid-60s, after working with the Democratic National Committee and the Johnson administration in Washington, Mrs. Bates had returned to Arkansas and was eventually appointed executive director of the Economic Opportunity Agency in the small southeast Arkansas town of Mitchellville, just 10 miles south of my home.

I was 16 years old when I came pitifully close to working for Mrs. Bates in 1969 . . . if only I had done better on her typing test. She had smiled, shaken her head and suggested: "Why don't you come back, and let's try again next summer." That next summer, however, I was lucky enough to get hired at the Lincoln County courthouse.

It wasn't until 1987 that I got a second chance to work for Mrs. Bates. A good friend and co-worker told me that Daisy Bates needed a managing editor at her newspaper. Earlier that summer, I'd told my friend Patsy I felt ready for a life change. She'd looked at me and rolled her eyes, reminding me that she'd heard it all before. I was serious this time, I told her. I was ready to entrench myself deeper into the world of writing.

"That's what I'm supposed to be doing. That's what I'll be doing for the rest of my life," I told her.

Patsy had laughed, still not convinced I was serious about leaving the Migrant Data Bank, where we'd worked together for six years.

"As I recall, you were going to stay here just three years. You've already been here six."

I enjoyed my job as director of information at the Migrant Data Bank. It was a fascinating organization, with the important task of maintaining and transferring migrant students' education and health records across the country as their parents moved to follow the seasonal farm jobs.

Working at the Migrant Data Bank afforded me a thorough orientation into the world and culture of migrant students and their families. Yet, I longed to do the kind of writing that didn't carry with it the stigma of government writing.

Writing was my calling. I'd known that for as long as I could remember. I'd begun trying my hand at it in elementary school. Unfortunately, there was no teacher and no one in the community I could talk to about writing as a career. Even the teachers who complimented me on my writing didn't go farther than those compliments. None mentioned or suggested a degree or career in writing or journalism.

I loved college life, but was far from the serious college student. For two years, in fact, I drifted between socializing and searching for the perfect major for a girl with no real interests except reading and writing.

It took me two years to figure out that I wouldn't make a good sociologist or counselor. I was already a junior before I realized that a journalism degree came closest to fitting my obsessions. At the time, the university had no writing degree.

I married my college sweetheart, Darryl Lunon, in June 1973. Our son, D.K., was born that fall. Incredibly, becoming a wife and mother suddenly transformed me into a serious student, anxious to complete my studies. I was more diligent than I'd been since arriving on the University of Arkansas campus.

While in the journalism program, I began freelancing for the *Grapevine*, a campus newspaper. And for the first time, my name appeared on the dean's list. In spite of that positive transformation, I would never encourage young women to try the triple-duty life of being a student, mother and wife all rolled into one. I was amazingly fortunate that it worked for me.

When Darryl and I moved to Little Rock in 1977, I worked briefly for county government, but early in 1978 I began working for state government. I remained a government worker for nine years.

During this time, I continued my creative writing—stories, poetry, plays. I even freelanced for a couple of local publications. The occasional articles and profiles allowed me a byline and the opportunity to keep my foot in the door of "real" writing. In the end, though, the freelancing wasn't enough. I was obsessed with the need to try my hand at writing full time.

"I'm serious this time, Patsy . . . it's time. I'm leaving this year."

Patsy just nodded, as if she wouldn't even give it a second thought. But, a few days later, she buzzed my office.

"I just heard that Daisy Bates needs a managing editor for her weekly newspaper."

The newspaper's managing editor was leaving to attend law school, Patsy told me, as I stood in her door that morning. Patsy had hardly slipped me the contact name and phone number before I thanked her and slipped quickly through her door.

I closed my office door before sitting down to dial the number to the *Arkansas State Press*. No answer. I left my name, number and a brief message about my interest in the upcoming job vacancy. I spent much of the rest of that afternoon doctoring the resume I hadn't looked at in six years. Now I needed to make certain it would fit the position.

Don Trimble, managing editor at the *Arkansas State Press*, called me the next day and asked if I could come in that evening for an interview. I took my revised resume with me. Don spent an hour talking with me about the duties of the job. Before I left, he promised to talk with Mrs. Bates and get back with me within the next couple of days.

Don called the next day and asked if I could return for a second interview. This time Mrs. Bates would be interviewing me.

"Of course. What time?" I asked. I was far more excited than I let on. I was also far more nervous about this second interview.

I hadn't seen Mrs. Bates since that summer day back in 1969. I certainly was hoping for a different outcome this time. I now wished I'd asked Don more questions and knew exactly what Mrs. Bates was looking for. I tried staying positive, telling myself I had a lot of experience, that I was actually a pretty good writer . . . plus, I was good at doing all kinds of "duties as assigned."

When I arrived, a few minutes early, Mrs. Bates was talking with someone. Don greeted me and suggested I wait at his desk until she was ready for me. When she finished, he motioned to me to go and take a seat at her desk. Don brought a seat with him and sat opposite us. As Mrs. Bates smiled, I couldn't help but remember that day almost 20 years earlier.

"Well, how are you, Miss Lunon?"

My breath caught. Don obviously thought I already knew, or he forgot to tell me that Mrs. Bates' speech was impaired. I was grateful that he was there, helping out whenever my face showed him I couldn't decipher her words. As we talked, her speech became easier for me to understand. Don would later tell me that Mrs. Bates had had a number of strokes that affected her speech.

"It's actually gotten better over the last couple of years," he said. I apologized that I seemed so lost during part of our interview. He said he understood.

Thankfully, I must have answered enough questions correctly. Don called the next day to tell me the job was mine, if I still wanted it. I was jumping for joy in my mind and heart, but simply said, "Yes, I do . . . when do I start?" I was certain that fate was on my side.

I gave my obligatory two-week notice at the Migrant Data Bank the very next day. I used much of those two weeks preparing for my transformation, including spending a couple of hours each evening at the *Arkansas State Press*, shadowing Don as he went through his daily activities.

By the end of August, I had said goodbye to the Migrant Data Bank and the friends I'd made there and ensconced myself in my new role as managing editor of Arkansas' oldest and most popular black newspaper.

Slowly, but surely, I was gaining an understanding of this strange, new world of weekly newspaper publishing.

Don jokingly reminded me during his last days at the newspaper that serving as Daisy Bates' managing editor would definitely include some "duties as necessary." He seemed delighted to be inching closer each day out the newspaper's door, and I was more than a little sad to see him go so soon.

While my role at the newspaper involved the more common tasks of news reporting, interviewing, editing, layout and photography—including learning to develop my own photos—my "extra" duties called for human resource responsibilities, marketing, advertising and everyday office maintenance. Within days, I was questioning what all had I gotten myself into?

As excited as I was about this new chapter in my life, my excitement was tempered by the loss of my sister, Jo Ann. We had buried her just two weeks before I took the job at the newspaper. My joy and excitement were mixed with more than a little grief.

From that day forward, whenever I remembered my first days at the *Arkansas State Press*, the memory was intermingled with the loss of my sister. Two weeks wasn't nearly enough time for me to grieve or come to terms with such a loss.

The uncanny thing was that these two huge personalities were so much alike. Both Daisy Bates and Jo Ann had beautiful and bold personalities, though they were completely different physically. Jo Ann was dark-complexioned and statuesque, while Mrs. Bates was very fair-skinned and petite. Both, however, were brilliant, charming, opinionated, and sometimes painfully blunt.

On the one hand, the timing of my taking the managing editor position was perfect. I was grateful for the new role for much the same reason as I was bothered by it. The challenge of learning how to run the small newspaper helped me work through my grief and sadness.

Mrs. Bates needed me to perform, and my grief and mourning were something I had to deal with on my own time. The mourning would have to come in the wee hours of the night when I slipped home and into my bed, barely taking the time to hug my son and apologize for this new life I'd pulled him into.

Even though I hadn't seen Mrs. Bates since I was 16 years old, I was well aware of the history of the *Arkansas State Press* and of Mrs. Bates and her husband, L.C., who co-founded the newspaper in 1941. I knew the critical role they had played in helping to educate and inform black Arkansans and Americans in general about the injustices taking place in our state. I had a special pride and admiration for what these two amazing people had done for the state and the role the newspaper played in American history.

Much water had passed under the bridge since the 1957 crisis in which federal troops were sent in to enforce integration at Little Rock's all-white Central High School, and Daisy and L.C. Bates' loss of the newspaper two years later. It was common knowledge that white advertisers, who didn't agree with the Bates' politics or their newspaper's editorials and articles, pulled their ads from the newspaper in 1959.

Before L.C. passed away in 1980, Mrs. Bates promised him she would somehow revive the newspaper. She kept her promise, and in 1984 the *Arkansas State Press* came back with a bang. Everyone agreed that the revival of the newspaper—nearly 30 years after the '57 integration crisis—was a brave and courageous effort.

In truth, 30 years was a long time. Not only was Mrs. Bates almost 30 years older and in poor health, but also the black community had changed. And though many of the problems voiced in the early newspaper remained, the black community had now chosen to deal with them differently.

During its heyday in the '40s and '50s, the *Arkansas State Press* had been recognized both locally and nationally for its hard-hitting, brave reporting.

For good or bad, the world of journalism in the black community had changed; and most newspapers had transformed themselves out of the pre-civil rights era style of advocacy journalism, the kind that Daisy and L.C. Bates and so many other great black newspaper publishers had perfected.

It wasn't just the newspaper format and content that had changed by 1984. Most small newspapers were struggling to stay above water, to maintain advertisers and readerships.

Thus, while there was excitement around the return of the *Arkansas State Press* and nostalgia for what it meant to the black community, the truth was that it could never again play the role it had in the '40s and '50s.

Mrs. Bates' health was an important part of that change, as were her advanced age and her energy level. Her desire was as strong as ever, but there was a limit to her involvement.

The community's commitment to the paper's revival was heartfelt. There was moral support from the black community as well as some from the white community. But there wasn't an outpouring of much-needed financial support.

When I first met Mrs. Bates in Mitchellville in 1969, my first thought was how odd that someone with her amazing history, a woman who looked as if she had stepped out of a *Vogue* magazine, was directing a jobs program out of a trailer house in a small town like Mitchellville.

I was, more than anything, humbled by this famous woman who had such a large and giving heart. When we met again nearly 20 years later, I was still amazed by this inimitable and beautiful woman. It was an exciting opportunity for me. Daisy Bates was an Arkansas icon . . . and still my idol. To work for her was a great honor.

During the early months of my new career, I dealt with more than a little guilt. I'd changed my life around just as my son was going into his teen years. We had always enjoyed a close relationship. His father and I had stayed involved in his school and extracurricular activities. This new career would change that.

Though I promised myself I'd stay involved, it was physically impossible with the demands of the newspaper. Anyone who has ever worked for a small newspaper knows about those demands. Anyone who has worked for a small, struggling black newspaper knows that the demands are threefold.

As managing editor, my job was as much about doing tasks "as deemed necessary," as it was about managing the newspaper. We needed all hands on deck to get the newspaper out each week, and very often the deck was short on hands.

Small newspapers are known for high turnover rates, unfortunately. Once an editor or reporter or photographer learns the ropes, they are more likely than not, already preparing their exit strategies and seeking work at larger, more lucrative newspapers. Small, struggling newspapers like ours could never compete in that realm.

Around the third month, I was beginning to understand just how hard my job really was. I was determined to do the best job I could and to make Mrs. Bates proud of me. I often joked with friends that none of my 10 years of chopping cotton were as exhausting or demanding. We never had to get to the field before the sun was up or stay there after the sun went down. That was not the case with the newspaper.

In the five months between August 1987 and January 1988, I went from a new managing editor just hitting her stride in learning the ropes of running a small, struggling newspaper to the incredible challenge of owning it.

I'll never forget the day Mrs. Bates called me to her desk and told me the shocking news: "I'm tired, and I've decided I'm going home."

I can only imagine the expression on my face. The initial shock was closely followed by fear and disappointment. There was also a bit of irrational anger—some directed at Mrs. Bates, but mostly at myself. I'd taken this giant step outside my comfort zone and now look where it had gotten me.

What was I supposed to do now that I had walked away from a safe state government job? I wanted to ask Mrs. Bates.

As I returned to my desk, I was trying to convince myself that the giant leap I'd taken was still what I was supposed to do . . . that this job really was worth the plunge. The nagging worry was in knowing how much of an impact the drastic change in my work schedule was having on my relationship with my son.

I hadn't taken the managing editor position with any thoughts of moving beyond that role. In fact, way back in the crevices of my brain, I was thinking of that magic number of three years, that by then I'd be ready to move on to something even more in line with a life of writing. Little did I know or guess that way back in Daisy Bates' mind was that it was time to walk away from this dream she had revived to keep a promise to her husband.

I shouldn't have been surprised or angry that she was retiring. It was obvious that her health was not good. Yet, she was still coming into the newspaper each morning like clockwork and staying all day. Her health, I knew, wouldn't improve as long as she kept up this regimen.

Mrs. Bates was 84, and you didn't have to be around her long to know that, in spite of that beautiful bright smile, she was both tired and burned out. What's more, she had given the newspaper her best shot and made herself sicker in the process.

Working at a newspaper ranks among the top most stressful careers, and people with health problems should not set foot inside ne.

I was not Mrs. Bates' first choice to take over the newspaper. In fact, the last thing she would have expected was my inquiry into purchasing it, in the end. She had other offers, and she interviewed some of those people right there in the office.

As I worked diligently in the weeks before my own final decision, I was toying with the idea of returning to state government, or seeking other employment. I just wasn't interested in working under another publisher. Working for Mrs. Bates meant something special to me. It wouldn't be the same if someone else came in and took over.

I was a fool for risks, obviously. Here I was, again, making life-changing decisions that were based on what my heart told me was the right thing for me. Again, I would have to gain the confidence and support of my husband and son. Later, when I decided it could actually happen I'd have to ask for help from two of my siblings.

I'm not so sure that dreamers don't think more with their hearts, than their brains. However, I'm sure—whether it's good or bad—logic does not always play as important a part in my decision-making process, as it does with most people.

In December 1987, four months after I'd walked into the *Arkansas State Press* to interview for the managing editor position, the newspaper changed ownership—from the hands of my idol and mentor, Mrs. Daisy Bates, to my trembling hands. I knew I was biting off much more than I'd ever meant to when I first walked into the newspaper. But three months later, that little voice inside was telling me things were as they should be.

Newspaper publishing turned out to be both more exciting and more challenging than I would have ever imagined. I loved the work. I worked harder than I would have imagined, but ours was a small operation and I was the owner. Owners of small businesses almost always work twice as hard as anyone who works for them. I didn't mind. I had been given an amazing opportunity, a gift.

What I never wanted to fool myself about was that Mrs. Bates and I were one and the same. I was not a younger, more energetic Daisy Bates. I would never, ever be able to fit into her size five shoes. I could never earn the label civil rights and newspaper legend she had come to earn. She had suffered more for those titles than I ever would. She had paid her dues.

Yet, I was proud and grateful that I could stand on my hero's shoulders. As narrow and tiny as they were, they were formidable. Daisy Bates had proven that women could do great things with courage and stamina and persistence. I could never thank her enough for that lesson. She was a wonderful example of what women had contributed to the civil rights struggle. Truthfully, there were far too few women honored in that arena.

The *Arkansas State Press* would continue to contribute information about our people, our community, our injustices and our needs. No, we weren't writing about civil rights marches or governors standing in the doorways of white schools to keep blacks out or regular and overt racial discrimination, but we would still write about the issues that had an impact on all of us every day.

I was fully aware, however, of the segments of the community that felt something had been lost when the newspaper changed hands. Though I believed the greatest loss had taken place in 1959 when the Bates were forced to close the paper, I understood that for many, the *Arkansas State Press* without Daisy Bates was no longer the *Arkansas State Press*. She and her husband symbolized the struggle, something many people didn't want to forget.

No, the newspaper would never be the same, for lots of reasons. The change from a pre-civil rights-era newspaper to a post-civil rights newspaper meant that it was less hard-hitting and had a less aggressive style of reporting than what the Bates and other black newspaper publishers were known for in the '40s and '50s.

As much as I admired L.C. and Daisy Bates, we were different people and different types of communicators. I was no Daisy Bates, and I would never be an icon. I was following in her footsteps, but at the same time trying to forge some of my own.

I had my own idea of the direction in which the newspaper should be moving, and I was working very hard to push it in that direction. I never doubted that Mrs. Bates was wise enough to see what I was trying to do and compassionate enough to appreciate my slightly different sense of direction for the newspaper.

Looking back on that amazing period in my life, I learned two things about myself: 1) In spite of the remarkable history of the *Arkansas State Press*, had I been someone who consistently responded to what my brain, rather than my heart, told me, I never would have taken such a step out on faith in the first place. 2) Most decisions I would make in life would be a balancing act. Going for my dreams was as important to me as breathing, but that would always mean giving up a little or a lot of my comfort zone.

My decision to purchase the newspaper was one I would never regret, though I would always wish it had come without changes in the rest of my life. The newspaper experience had a wonderful and positive impact on my life. Most importantly, it allowed me to live my dream and to become more than an admirer, but also a friend of a woman who meant so much to me.

I also quickly learned that the day-to-day operation of a small, black-owned paper would be a challenge. There simply weren't an overwhelming number of financially lucrative small newspapers in the country, especially those owned by blacks or minorities. Anyone looking to make a profit, or to even keep a consistent balance in a bank account, might want to try another line of work.

I was always grateful for the periods when the newspaper broke even, allowing for small reserves in the bank and affording us the opportunity to implement new projects. We were able to nurture and maintain some important advertisement relationships, both within the state and nationally.

Returning advertisers are every small publisher's dream, and many great daily newspapers as well as small weekly newspapers like the *Arkansas State Press* had been forced to close their doors when advertisers chose not to return.

I was, admittedly, surprised to learn in 1987 that, in spite of Arkansas' reverence for Mrs. Bates, the newspaper's financial standings didn't bear that out. Even so, I wasn't about to change my mind. I was simply put on notice as to what challenges lay ahead for me.

None of this, I soon learned, was unique to me or Mrs. Bates or the *Arkansas State Press*. I became intimately involved in the National Newspaper Publishers Association—made up of black newspaper publishers around the country—and I quickly learned that most black newspapers were experiencing the very challenges that confronted me, and certainly Mrs. Bates before me. The uphill battles were part of the territory for small, independent newspapers, I was told, more often than I wanted to hear.

Beyond constantly courting advertisers, black newspapers also have the gargantuan task of convincing the community that there is a need for taking 30 minutes each day to read a newspaper.

When newspapers flourish, it is greatly thanks to a healthy advertisement clientele, but it is also because they have a healthy, consistent readership and subscribers' list.

It was a plus that I was neither expectant, nor energized by great financial returns. I absolutely enjoyed publishing the newspaper, and I believed I was making a contribution to our community.

I enjoyed writing weekly editorials and sometimes feature stories. I enjoyed seeing the first copies off the press each Wednesday and being the first to read each issue before the rest of our readership did. I could either brace myself if there were blatant errors or breathe a sigh of relief when there weren't.

While being a small newspaper publisher didn't automatically place me in the movers and shakers category, there were some perks. I learned a great deal about what was going on in the city and the state. Being a newspaper publisher allowed me my first certificate in politics 101.

It was during those years that I cut my teeth on local and state politics, something I frankly hadn't paid much attention to since moving to Little Rock. There were endless opportunities to cover local political stories, to meet and interview political leaders and to gain their wisdom and opinions on the issues, big and small.

Mrs. Bates had agreed to continue to come into the office when she felt up to it. She served as a consultant and rarely missed a day for the next year. She would arrive around midmorning and remain until the end of the day. I loved having her there, and was grateful for the benefit of her wisdom and experience. It wasn't long before my adulation settled into something closer to friendship.

In 1990, we decided to move the newspaper from its original site in the Village Square strip mall at 16th and Izard to a small bungalow at 17th and Broadway. I had always liked the Quapaw Quarters area near downtown Little Rock. My five employees were ecstatic. They loved having more work space and the feeling of security in the new location. Always an early riser, I found the drive down Broadway Street before 7 a.m. calming. It helped me prepare myself for the day.

I was buried in my work at the newspaper, but not so much that I didn't notice how D.K. had magically morphed from an adolescent to a wonderfully confident and handsome young man. D.K. was in high school, and a lot of our conversations were about his college plans. My son had been set on becoming a "Morehouse Man" since he was in junior high school. Already, we were discussing options about how we could make sure he got to Atlanta's Morehouse College.

He had finally become accustomed to my crazed work hours and my new career. He came to the office in the evenings to help out, when he wasn't involved in extracurricular activities at his school.

It was a life I'd chosen for myself, but it was very important that my son felt comfortable with that life, too. It was only when I felt he had accepted my career that I was 100 percent sure I had made the right choice.

⁂

July 1992 was an exciting time for Arkansas and for me. The state had been blessed with one of the smartest and most effective young governors in the country for 11 years; and that month, he was nominated as the Democrats' presidential candidate. There's not much that could be more exciting for our small, rural state.

It hadn't been many years ago that a survey showed that most CEOs of Fortune 500 companies didn't know where Arkansas was on the map.

The *Arkansas State Press* was busy running stories about this historic time for our state, and we put out special issues on the people we knew were involved in the presidential campaign. I was already having visions of what it would be like for our small newspaper once Governor Bill Clinton became President Bill Clinton.

The fact that a presidential campaign was taking place right down the street from our newspaper was sometimes hard to fathom. We had temporary residents from all over the country living and working in our town during this historic campaign. Many of them would soon become household names: James "Ragin' Cajun" Carville, George Stephanopoulos, Dee Dee Myers, Maggie Williams, and many others.

Admittedly, it was a good time to be publisher of the *Arkansas State Press*. Campaign seasons are always lucrative ad times for newspapers, but a presidential campaign in our own backyard? The excitement wasn't just that we would be getting campaign ads, but our newspaper might very well have access to the White House, a special media relationship with the presidency.

I very often arrived at my newspaper office during the same time that Governor Clinton jogged past our office on Broadway Street. We'd exchange hellos and sometimes brief niceties. After the nomination, it became extremely likely that, come November, those exchanges might be just fond memories. He might very well be jogging somewhere around the White House in Washington.

Even the Arkansans who didn't especially take to Bill Clinton as governor were more excited than they really wanted to admit. In spite of their political differences with him, he was our own—our native son. More importantly, he was well on his way to being the first Arkansan ever to be elected president. It was truly a time of hope and possibilities, and we—both blacks and whites—were swept up by it all.

I attended my very first Democratic National Convention in July 1992. The convention was another one of those events I'd heard about most of my adult life, but one in which I'd never personally participated.

Being at the convention and witnessing our very own governor being announced as the presidential nominee were the best possible ways to fall in love with the Democratic process at the national level. Thousands of men and women, all just as excited as I was, waved their American flags, held up their nominee's signs, and yelled out their states. I had never witnessed, nor imagined, such excitement around politics

There were thousands of people at the convention, held in New York City's Madison Square Garden, that night. They were all hyped up on hope and change for America; and our own Bill Clinton, along with his running mate Al Gore, were the agents of that change.

While I was far too excited after returning home to Little Rock to describe the experience and my emotions to anyone, I knew my political thermometer had gone from lukewarm to hot in those few days. I was fired up about the whole democratic political process.

I had grown up pretty much a political cynic, thanks to my father who loved politics, but spared no slack for most politicians. In July 1992, I became convinced that politics was not only an important part of our lives, but good politics could also change our lives and the status quo.

You can imagine, then, how moved I was by the convention. It forced me to skip the getting-my-feet-wet stage of politics and moved me on to a complete immersion.

I was certain that I must play a role in the presidential campaign. I wanted to be a part of the history that I knew in my bones was about to be made. I had already talked myself into taking a sabbatical from my newspaper leading up to the election, if my wish became reality.

I wasn't the only one convinced during that convention. So many of us returned to Arkansas with the same realization—that this can really happen . . . our Bill Clinton might actually be the next president of the United States.

To be fair, many of us never doubted that he was presidential material. And we tempered our own excitement about the possibilities based on the rest of the country's lack of knowledge.

My own brothers, and many other young law students who came to know Bill and Hillary Clinton as law professors at the University of Arkansas in the mid-70s, sensed the potential for greatness in Bill Clinton.

Students and faculty, even then, were discussing this young lawyer's incredible brilliance and political savvy. That perception heightened during Bill Clinton's 11 years as governor, as we watched him confront the historical racial and social ills of our state and begin to make a difference.

By the time the rest of the world finally took notice of Bill Clinton in1992, not only had all the attributes I'd admired 14 years earlier gelled, but also there was so much more political substance to him by then. More importantly, he had nearly12 years of real accomplishments under his belt.

I was swept up in the country's and Arkansas' excitement. And, as I promised myself just days after returning from the convention, I began asking questions about how I could work with the Clinton-Gore Campaign. I was ready and willing to offer my services.

And it turned out that I would. In July, I took a sabbatical from my beloved newspaper for the four months leading up to the November election. I would play a small part in this historical change for the country. I was absolutely convinced Bill Clinton would be good for America, and his presidency would be good for Arkansas.

I was brought into the campaign's press office, where I worked with a young woman by the name of Avis LaVelle, a former press secretary to Chicago Mayor Richard M. Daley. Most people never realized that

Avis served as one of two media spokeswomen for the Clinton-Gore campaign. Dee Dee Myers, however, was the name most people recognized as the press secretary for the campaign.

My role in the press office was to coordinate minority media outreach with African American and other minority media across the country. I was assisted by two young women: one, a Chicago native, and the other, an Arkansan.

While this job was a full eight hours, and even more from time to time, I continued to spend a few late hours at the newspaper. That was possible most days. When it didn't work out, I resumed weekend office hours at the *State Press*. I kept telling myself that this juggling act would end in November.

August 1992 was a different kind of milestone. D.K. had graduated from Central High School in May and worked through that summer. By August, he was preparing to go off to Morehouse—the college he'd dreamed of attending for years. I couldn't count how many times he had reminded me of the many great Americans who happened to also be alumni of Morehouse, including the Reverend Martin Luther King Jr.

I was excited, proud, and an emotional mess. While there are good reasons for having just one child, as my empty-nest days grew closer, I was questioning the wisdom of that decision.

Our home on Vancouver Drive would serve as little more than a bed-and-breakfast where I slept and sometimes ate. No more daily doses of D.K.'s lively, uplifting personality. No more of our grown-up chats. I would also miss having his best friends, Cameron and Tony, hanging out at our home. They were wonderful young men who I'd come to love as if they were the two other sons I never had.

I was ecstatic to learn that Cameron was also attending Morehouse, and saddened to learn that Tony was not. I was proud, though, that Tony was going to a great school like Southern Methodist University in Dallas.

Even though my life was busier than ever, D.K. and I were still able to squeeze in some quality time to talk about what was going on in our lives, and about world issues. Unlike my own childhood of shy and quiet observations, my son was a confident communicator and always had questions and observations he wanted to share. I was glad Darryl and I had encouraged that.

As exciting as this giant step would be for D.K., I imagined he must have been a little scared, too. College was a huge change from the safety and security of living at home with Mama and attending a school with teenagers, most of whom you knew by first name.

Though he would never have admitted it, D.K. had grown up fairly sheltered. Even after I began working the crazy newspaper hours, we stayed connected. I was confident that who he was had already been etched into his being in those early childhood years—before the big changes in our lives, before my divorce from his father, before the newspaper or the campaign came along.

I'd watched with both nostalgia and awe as D.K. had changed from a child who loved hanging out with his mother to one who preferred hanging out with friends, then girlfriends. Now I was watching him prepare to completely disengage from the "us" that was so important to me.

His metamorphosis, while awesome to watch, was also a lot more painful and scary than I ever let on. I imagined my once full life would now be filled with holes.

Looking back, I wish I had captured those moments leading up to my son's leaving home in pictures. He would never be there again, teetering between childhood and adulthood. That was a time to savor.

Unfortunately, D.K.'s departure was that very important thing wedged between my very hectic life as I divided my time between the campaign and the newspaper. I wasn't able to shut my brain off to what was going on in either one, as we prepared for D.K.'s big move.

I had begun dating Bob Nash a year earlier, in 1991. Bob and I had known each other for years. Our children had attended the same schools at one point, and his former wife and I belonged to the same women's organization.

It turned out that Bob and I both ended up single around the same time, and what had been a platonic friendship for years morphed into something more.

Bob had worked for Governor Clinton as a senior economic aide for eight of Bill Clinton's nearly 12 years as governor. Then he became director of the Arkansas Finance and Development Agency.

By 1992, Bob was a fairly constant fixture in D.K.'s and my life. I was grateful beyond words when he offered to drive us down to Morehouse College.

What's more, he offered use of his van. D.K. and I spent a few harried evenings cleaning out his bedroom, packing what seemed like everything he'd ever need—clothing, music stereo, bedding and loads of other things—into Bob's van.

We left for Atlanta after work on a Friday evening. While I knew the drive would take 10 hours, I didn't realize what a long 10 hours it would be. We made one pit stop for gas and restroom use.

It was the longest, darkest, loneliest highway I'd ever experienced, including the dark dirt roads of southeast Arkansas. We were two hours outside Atlanta when we saw a huge Shoney's restaurant sign. All of our stomachs must have growled at the same time.

The drive couldn't be described as fun by any stretch of the imagination. I was feeling a little guilty, too, knowing that Bob could have been home sleeping or at least in his own space. All of us were tired, sleepy and pretty silent by the time we drove into Atlanta.

The cramped drive brought out D.K.'s seldom-seen grouchiness. I had to constantly remind myself that my son was a teenager, even though he didn't often exhibit the normal teen angst. Being stuck inside a car with two grown-ups for 10 hours couldn't be his idea of fun, either.

Finally, we arrived at the campus and asked a security guard for directions to the registration office. We had already decided this would be a turnaround trip for us. We spent approximately four hours on the campus, and most of that time was spent in line at the registration office.

I was sad that I wouldn't spend any real time with D.K during this very important trip. Our togetherness was spent in lines, in one office, then another. We were both too stressed to think about how we were missing out on quality time.

Thanks to my wonderful friend E. Lynn Harris, D.K. had participated in one of The Coca-Cola Company's summer enrichment programs for minority students two years earlier. He had been flown to Atlanta and placed in a Morehouse dorm for one week.

He had come back even more convinced that Morehouse was the place for him. I'm sure, in his teenager's excitement about being away from home, he hadn't paid attention to the dorms.

So, even though he knew what to expect, I didn't. Yet, I can't imagine my thoughts were all that different. I am sure they were in line with other parents who drop their sons or daughters off at fine, historical colleges and universities and wonder why can't the schools afford nicer dorms for their students?

In all fairness, I am sure there is some well-studied reasoning behind the uniformly unattractiveness of dorm rooms, especially those set aside for new college students.

I quickly learned that limited parking space, like the endless lines at the registrar's office, is a problem that transcend all college campuses—be they historically black or predominantly white. Most of our short time on the campus was spent searching for a legal place to park as we transferred D.K.'s bedroom furniture, clothing and stereo up the stairs of his dorm and into his small room.

None of us was in a great mood by the time we'd finally unloaded and moved all of his belongings to his room. By then, we were all sick of each other. D.K. was anxious to find his friends. We were tired, but also anxious to get started on our 10-hour drive back down that long, dark highway to Little Rock.

D.K.'s and my goodbyes were not the kind that drew looks of embarrassment from onlookers. I was trying very hard to be grown-up about this change in my life and to ignore the big hole left by his going away to college. I held my tears at bay and refused to embarrass him or myself with the gnashing and wailing I felt inside.

What mother can stand the idea of leaving her baby on a strange campus, full of strange teachers, and even stranger children? I wasn't sure, but I imagined D.K. was ready to get on with his new life, and he needed me to say a final goodbye so that he could get started.

D.K. had grown up in a place where most people knew him and his parents. Here, he was just one more student and from a place even Georgians looked down on.

Most of his high school instructors had liked him. He'd gotten to know most of them well enough to drop by their offices or classrooms to chat outside of class. All of his college teachers would be strangers and maybe not see how special he was.

As Bob and I drove off the historic campus, I prayed with all my heart that this would be a wonderful experience for my son. He deserved it, but most importantly, I was grateful beyond words that his youthful dreams to one day become a "Morehouse Man" were on their way to becoming a reality.

Election night 1992 is still a blur to me. Few, if any, campaign workers got more than two uninterrupted hours of sleep. The younger campaign workers likely got no sleep.

We spent most of the night shuffling between the campaign headquarters and the Little Rock Convention Center—the place to be on election night and the site of most of the election action. There were luminaries milling around downtown Little Rock and hundreds more in their rooms at the two major downtown hotels—the Excelsior and the Capitol Hotel.

Around midnight, crowds began to make their way to the front yard of the Old State House where the newly elected president was about to make his victory speech. There was an endless sea of people . . . too many to fit comfortably into the block long space around the stage.

When the president-elect, his wife Hillary, and their 13-year-old daughter Chelsea walked out onto the stage, there likely was not one silent voice in the city. Hoots and cheers, cowboy yells, African ululations, and even something akin to wails burst from the wildly excited crowd.

How could Bill Clinton not give a moving speech in response to such a rousing show of love and adulation? Even those of us too tired to hold our heads up or to stand on our two feet one minute earlier continued to stand and scream along with the rest of the crowd of mesmerized loyalists.

It was a heart-felt speech, one that brought most of his campaign aides to tears. One look around told me that both men and women were wiping at tears of joy and disbelief.

Bill Clinton's familiar "God Bless America" was immediately followed by a party yell that could only come out of Arkansas. The partying would continue through the streets of Little Rock until the wee, wee hours of the morning.

While the heart and spirit were willing, my body absolutely was not. I simply was not a teeny-bopper or 20-something anymore. Without a few hours of sleep, I would never be able to make it into the campaign headquarters the next morning at a respectable hour. And the next day would be a very busy one for the Clinton-Gore Campaign.

Those of us who actually got a few hours of sleep arrived in the campaign office between 9 and 10 a.m. That's late in the world of campaign headquarters, but it was the best our poor bodies could do.

Anyone who has ever worked a presidential campaign knows that the day after Election Day, especially for the winner, is even more hectic than the day of the election. The press office was a madhouse.

Not only was election night a blur, but the next days were as well. The office was going crazy with hurried plans to transport the campaign from the Gazette building over to the virtually new bank building on Main Street. Within a matter of hours, we were transformed from the Clinton-Gore Campaign to the Clinton-Gore transition office.

My plans since joining the campaign had been to stick around through the election, then return to my real life, the newspaper. But November 8, the day after the election, was so wild that I didn't once think about that plan.

Besides, the Clinton-Gore press people needed every hand they could get. No one asked if I was going on to the transition office that next morning, but simply included me on the list of staff that would become part of the transition office. I was still caught up in the excitement and too busy to query myself about this breach in self-promises.

By the end of the week, I conceded that this made sense. The transition office would need me at least as much as the campaign headquarters had. I would remain through the presidential transition and return to the newspaper in January, when the rest of the team disbursed and the president-elect went on to Washington.

I began making plans to return to the newspaper within the next two months. On the evening of November 8, I had gone to the newspaper to announce my temporary change in plans. To my surprise, the staff was so caught up in the excitement of the election that not only was my announcement anti-climatic, but it wasn't something my staff seemed the least bit upset about.

Josephine Rumph, my editor, paused briefly in her conversation with Arnold, a reporter, to say: "Janis, don't worry. We're doing fine. Besides, you're just a phone call away. We'll be right here when you get back."

While I did wonder whether I should worry that they seemed to be getting along just as well without me, I didn't have much time to worry about it. I, too, was still on my election high. The excitement of Bill Clinton winning the presidency was second only to the awe of being a part of that winning team—even in a small way. This excitement would remain with me for weeks.

Yet, even with all the afterglow of the campaign and the election, I came to a very sobering decision. I was not cut out for campaigns. Campaigns were a lot sexier, at least for me, if you're looking at them from the outside.

There were lots of people who would viscerally disagree. There were many campaign workers who absolutely loved the high intensity atmosphere of campaign work, not just the young, college students, but the political veterans who were my age or older. They ate, breathed and slept politics and campaign work.

By the end of the campaign, I was convinced campaigns were either in your blood or not. For many people, those who had worked in one campaign or another year after year, this was definitely so.

What I learned, gratefully, was the many ways I could support candidates and help them win elections, rather than being intimately involved in the everyday work inside campaign offices. In spite of my sobering assessment, I would always know beyond a shadow of a doubt how lucky and blessed I was to have had this amazing experience.

It was another one of those once-in-a-lifetime opportunities. I'd taken a chance, led by my heart, and made the right decision. I didn't know it then, but that decision would have an impact on my life in an unforeseeable way.

PART III

A CHAPTER IN AN UNFINISHED LIFE

(1993)

In early December, I sat at my desk in the Clinton-Gore transition office's press department—one big room with a couple of offices identified for work and storage. The downtown Little Rock bank building was now the Clinton-Gore presidential office.

In just a few days, I thought, I'd be back in my own corner office, sitting at my own desk at the *State Press*. The two extra months I'd tacked onto my sabbatical were passing quickly. We'd won, and as long as things were going relatively well at the newspaper, I didn't feel so guilty. But I was beginning to miss my life, my staff, and my corner office on Broadway Street.

I imagined what it must be like for the Bush Campaign. I was sure time wasn't passing half as fast. Each day must seem like a month for the losing candidate and his staff members who had to dismantle their campaign offices and return dejectedly to their real lives.

Sometime during the mid-morning, the press office intern stuck his head in my office doorway. "Dee Dee wants a meeting with all you people." I looked up from my desk at Bryan's smiling face. Before I could put the caller on hold and ask what the meeting was about, he'd disappeared.

I quickly ended my phone conversation with a newspaper reporter wanting photos sent "right away." Everybody wanted everything today or yesterday, I silently complained, pushing the photo file shut. I took a deep breath before walking across to Dee Dee Myers' office.

The 30-ish Myers was recently announced as President Clinton's White House press secretary.

"Grab a seat, guys . . . we need to go over a few things."

The White House press secretary-in-waiting joked for a while with the young staffers before pulling the single sheet of paper closer and clearing her throat.

Dee Dee had a talent for appearing laid back, while her rapid-fire speech told you there had to be some cogs inside, moving pretty darn fast. She didn't offer a lot of intense eye contact to the mostly young group of workers and volunteers.

She started out by thanking all of us for "giving up your lives for this campaign." She was gracious and grateful for our commitment and hard work during the transition period, but reminded us that the transition was quickly coming to an end.

There was nervous laughter and furtive glances around the room.

Dee Dee looked around the small office and said she had "some good news and not-so-good news." Some of us, she pointed out, would be given the option of coming to Washington and working in the White House, but most wouldn't.

"Unfortunately," she said, "there simply won't be enough positions to accommodate everyone."

I offered a half smile hoping to assure her that I was fine with that. Some of the younger staffers ducked their heads, mumbled jokes or struck pensive poses. I hadn't come to the campaign looking for any payback other than a new man sitting in the Oval Office.

In truth, I was plain naïve when it came to politics. I didn't know there was such a thing as a coveted White House list created just weeks before the new president took over the White House.

While some of the much younger campaign aides had been whispering about what roles they wanted to take in the administration, I was already divorcing myself from campaign mode, spending my evenings back at the newspaper.

I imagined it would take time for me to fall back into the groove at the newspaper. It would likely seem slow, compared to the excitement of campaign work. But it was a slow I looked forward to getting use to again. I was certain it wouldn't take more than a couple of weeks for the campaign high to fade.

As exciting as the world of campaign work was, I'd missed my quiet mornings at the newspaper. Those early mornings—before the small staff showed up—were my time to organize my day, to read the mainstream newspapers, to write and rewrite my weekly columns, to take a look at my phone call list and decide who needed a return call.

It was also when I worried about the newspaper's bottom line, worried about increasing advertising dollars, and addressed the mundane administrative work implicit in small, weekly newspaper publishing.

As Dee Dee spoke, I wondered who of this small group of Easterners would be on that short list of White House staff. I remembered reading how John Kennedy's White House was full of young aides. He fed off the energy and hope of young people in his White House.

Certainly Bill Clinton's White House would mirror, to some extent, the campaign's makeup of young, bright, energetic men and women. They'd certainly worked their tails off and deserved it.

The press office, maybe more than most others in the transition office, was made up of these demographics. These youngsters had brought the invaluable combination of boundless energy and blind loyalty that youth affords in the long-running and often hard-fought presidential campaign. They, too, had taken part in rewriting presidential and, yes, Arkansas history.

As Dee Dee was wrapping up, I snapped back to the meeting, pushing to the background any thoughts of my upcoming move back to the *Arkansas State Press*. Two weeks from now my days would begin and end in that comfortable corner office at 1700 Broadway. I'd resume my late-night chats with my son—a new college student at Morehouse, and my weekend visits with Daddy. More than anything, I'd missed the peaceful 90-minute drives to Varner Road.

After the short meeting, I returned to my temporary office and took care of the reporter's request. I spent most of the afternoon either mailing out or filing new Cabinet members' bios and news releases on their announcements. I searched for empty spaces to put the bulging files of campaign photos that would soon be transferred to the Clinton White House.

The next mornings and days were much the same, taking care of news media inquiries and boxing up the files and documents that would be shipped to the press office in Washington.

Just weeks before the transition office was set to close, I came in with the expectation of more of the same, plus spending some time boxing up the few personal things I'd brought to the campaign. I had also planned to leave the office early enough to drop by the newspaper to work for a few hours. I thought I might even stop by during my lunch break. Or should I just pick up a salad and Dr Pepper downtown?

As the questions rattled around in my head, the young intern showed up at my door again. There was the same wide grin.

"What's the smirky smile about this time, Bryan?" I joked. The boy's constant happy-go-lucky personality always amused me.

"Oh, nothing. Jeff just wants you to stop by his office . . ." He rushed off to catch the obnoxiously loud phones without ending his sentence.

Jeff Eller, a Florida boy wonder who was brilliant and completely nontraditional in the way he got things done, had been the communications guru for the Clinton Campaign. I hadn't had much interaction with him during the campaign, but he now shared the space with the press office.

I had no idea what Jeff wanted to talk with me about when I went to his office. But the real confusion took place after I left his office. As I walked back to my desk from my short chat with him, I was convinced I'd been shoved inside someone else's dream.

I sat at my desk for a while staring into nothing, trying to replay what had just happened. My hands shook as I reached for the phone. Maybe if I said it out loud it would make more sense, or the bubble would burst. I dialed my home number. Janetta, my sister and temporary roommate, wasn't home. I closed the door and walked in circles around the office. My brain was reeling crazily.

Jeff, the recently announced White House media affairs director, had nonchalantly wondered if I had given any thoughts to coming to the White House and, if so, what I might consider doing. He wanted me to write something up for him for the next day.

As I sat in his office, it suddenly dawned on me that no one would believe that—at almost 40 years old—I didn't understand the political quid pro quo most politicos took for granted. I had missed the simple equation between harsh campaign work and the plum White House and government jobs just waiting to be filled by presidential appointees.

Beyond the new experience of working for a campaign and a candidate I believed in, and the ultimate gratitude of being part of a victorious campaign, I simply wasn't expecting anything more.

Our very own governor, Bill Clinton, would be the 42nd president of the United States of America! And while those months working inside the campaign had been exciting ones, I really was looking forward to returning to my newspaper and my real world once all of this was over.

Maybe it was because politics had not been something I studied as a general rule. I was not a politician. In fact, I had to justify myself to my friends who wondered half jokingly how a newspaper publisher remained objective about politics while she worked for a politician.

My response, of course, was that I had temporarily divorced myself from the newspaper, technically speaking. I was not writing for the newspaper during my time at the campaign.

In fact, Josephine, my editor, pretty much ran things during my sabbatical. At least in my mind, I'd hung my journalist's hat on a peg with a clear conscious as I did my part to bring about change in American government.

I'd learned who Bill Clinton was about the same time as the rest of the University of Arkansas-Fayetteville campus had. He'd made a splash when he came on the scene in 1973 during my sophomore year at the university. And so had Hillary Rodham, his significant other. They were already a twosome that made those around them sit up and take notice.

The two new law professors were extremely popular, even though some dyed-in-the-wool Southerners jokingly called them Eastern hippies. Likely, they were referring to Bill and Hillary's Yale law degrees or they simply weren't aware that Bill Clinton was born in Hope, Arkansas, and grew up in Hot Springs . . . or that Hillary Rodham was a Midwesterner, born on the outskirts of Chicago.

All the rumors were that the two young law professors were brilliant. They certainly found themselves a loyal following among the best-and-the-brightest law students on the campus.

It wasn't until 1978, after Darryl, D.K. and I moved from Fayetteville to Little Rock, that I actually met Bill Clinton and Hillary Rodham. They were more than just an "item" by then. They were man and wife. Bill Clinton had already served as Arkansas' attorney general, and that year he won his first election as governor of Arkansas. That was the start of my and the rest of Arkansas' 12-year "Clinton Watch."

I met Bill Clinton during his first term as governor. My brother, Jesse, had been one of Professor Clinton's law students and was hired as an assistant attorney general during Bill Clinton's term as Arkansas Attorney General. When Bill Clinton was elected America's youngest governor in 1978, Jesse moved with him to the State Capitol.

That year, Jesse served as the governor's agency liaison to the state's Department of Local Services. I was employed there as assistant director of a CETA project geared toward helping local governments across the state. It was a great project that was founded by a creative young man from northwest Arkansas. Todd Larson would become a good friend and mentor over the years.

During his first months in office, the 35-year-old Governor Clinton was said to visit every state agency and department in the state of Arkansas. When he visited our department, he greeted and talked with most of the workers there, regardless of our status.

That was my first introduction to the famous Clinton charisma. Most of the female workers spent most of the afternoon, long after he'd gone on to his next stop, discussing Bill Clinton's good looks, charm and gift of gab. They literally had to be reminded that the young man was the governor of our state. Already, there was that indescribable aura surrounding Bill Clinton.

By 1992, after years of observing the charismatic young governor's policies and changes, I was convinced his slightly left of center common sense approach to change would make for a better America.

Actually, by then I was convinced that almost any change was better than the direction the country was going under George H. W. Bush. The Reagan years hadn't been good for most of the people I knew—mostly poor, working-class, lower middle-class or minorities. And the Bush years hadn't been much better.

So, not only was I ready for a political change to move the nation forward, I wanted to see someone in the White House who gave a heck about everyday people—the people who had suffered the most throughout the '80s.

After the November election, I was satisfied I'd done my part. I believed the White House would be in good hands, and I could use my newspaper to tout the changes our new president brought to fruition. Of course, I'd have a responsibility to remind him and the state of any promises he forgot, too. Even a small newspaper such as ours had that responsibility.

I wrote the proposal Jeff Eller had asked for and went in the next day to talk with him. He looked at my proposal and said it was great, but that he already had someone in mind for basically the same role. I nodded and said I understood. That settled it, I thought. Now, I wouldn't have to make this big choice.

By the end of our conversation, however, Jeff had offered me another position in the White House Office of Media Affairs. I was stunned and probably showed it. He suggested I think about it and come back with an answer on Monday.

My meeting with Jeff was suddenly real. It clearly affected my life plans. I liked the life I was living right here in Little Rock. I'd never sought a life anywhere else. My son, my father, my family and friends, my newspaper, my past and future were all tied to Little Rock and to Varner Road in Gould, Arkansas.

Bob Nash, the man I'd allowed myself to fall in love with—after devoting my life to the newspaper for almost five years—was also right here. As I started out the door that evening, heading for the newspaper, I realized my mind was too unsettled, thoughts were still running over themselves. I dialed my newspaper office and asked the secretary to get Josephine.

"Hey, Josephine . . . how's everything going?"

She went over the uneventful details of the day.

"Great. You don't really need me, and I really need to get home to take care of an emergency. If anything comes up, call me at home." I wasn't ready to share that emergency with Josephine. I rang home again, and Janetta answered.

The drive from downtown Little Rock to Vancouver Drive in southwest Little Rock wasn't yet a certifiable traffic jam. We wouldn't be on any national list, but there were already signs of growth, signs that something magnificent was about to happen to our state—something most of us wouldn't have imagined two years earlier.

That 15-minute drive left just enough time for a wrestling match inside my brain—questions and my weak responses angrily slamming against each other. Was a simple yes-or-no decision supposed to wreak so much havoc? Was my consternation a way of manufacturing a road block to my future?

I pressed determinedly down on the gas pedal and switched the radio station to one with classical music. Both D.K. and I had used the station as an antidote to sleepless nights. It had always worked like magic. It had also worked to calm my nerves, but this time it wasn't working.

I took a deep breath before taking those few steps between my front door and the kitchen. I needed to calm myself before talking with Janetta. The anxiety was slowly, gratefully, slipping away as I moved into the dining area.

Since childhood, when I'd spent my early mornings following Mama around as she serenely performed her daily kitchen routines, I'd found peace and calm inside the kitchens of homes.

Mama's kitchen was furnished with a large, black wood-burning stove; a long, wooden table; and enough sturdy hardwood chairs to accommodate 10 or 12 Kearney children at a time.

My modern kitchens, though worlds different from Mama's, nevertheless represented the same sense of security, comfort and warmth my mother's kitchen always offered.

Janetta sat that evening at the glass dining room table that took up much of the small dining area. My small family had rarely used the table for dining. It was more of a stopping place, a conversation site. Most of its use, during our 15 years in the home, was during company visits. The table still sat in the very spot—next to the glass door leading to our backyard—where we'd placed it when we moved into the house in 1977.

The dining room was the perfect spot for early morning coffee and daydreams; where I could watch the rabbits or squirrels or, for a short time, D.K.'s small, white puppy run across the yard. Now, more than anything, it was Janetta's and my meeting place to recoup the day or stroll down memory lane or have political discussions that had grown considerably more passionate during the last months.

Janetta looked as elegant sitting at the table shelling and eating pecans, as she would have sitting inside Sotheby's auction house or the Kentucky Derby winner's circle. My sister is one of those women blessed with an inbred sophistication and elegance that remain firmly in place no matter where she happens to be or whether she's wearing an Armani suit or a cotton shift.

A glass bowl that likely started out brimming with pecans sat half full in the center of the table. I wasn't sure who loved pecans more, but Janetta was home more often, so I decided she was the culprit behind the disappearing pecans.

The sliding glass door doubled as a picture window to a spacious, but almost bare backyard. During our marriage, Darryl had attempted a garden in the backyard for several years. We waited and watched for the tomatoes and cucumbers he planted to grow to maturity, but, sadly, they never did.

During one of my parents' weekend visits, Daddy had walked out into the backyard and returned with a wry smile on his face.

"I hope you not expecting to raise vegetables out there . . . you wasting your time. That ground is pure buckshot. Nothing will ever grow out there."

We should have known. No matter how much grass seed we planted, the yard never filled in and always grew unevenly and patchy.

There was an old oak tree that stood in the middle of the unattractive yard. Though it had probably seen its best days, it still offered ample shade during the hot summers. On my most nostalgic days, the oak tree reminded me of the big walnut tree I'd loved so much down on Varner Road.

"How was your day? And what's got you so wound up?" Janetta asked, as she slipped from the chair to make tea.

I often wondered how Janetta could maintain her regal bearing through the various episodes of her life, when each episode in my own life seemed to affect me so differently. She didn't slouch or droop like I did when life dumped on me or I caught a lump on the head right out of the clear blue sky.

My sister had spent a lot of her early years in California and some in Hawaii—two places where healthy living was a way of life. Unfortunately, for those of us who had never left Arkansas, health was important, but not a requirement to join any club.

Janetta settled back at the table, waiting for the squeal of the teapot to tell her the water was boiling. I searched the refrigerator for a cold Dr Pepper. After finding one, I pushed the refrigerator door closed and popped the tab before sliding into the chair across from my sister.

It wasn't until then, the very moment I sat facing Janetta at the table, that I realized just how wound up I really was. Besides it being a long day, the pressure to make choices always stressed me out. Janetta half grinned and shook her head.

We had fallen easily into this after-work ritual of chats about what was going on with family members, the rest of the world, and what our politicians needed to do about an issue. We found humor in revisiting old stories about Varner Road. Now I was adding in something that felt as big and overwhelming as another world conflict for us to tackle. Should I or shouldn't I ditch my old, comfortable life and try on a new one for size?

What was usually as simple as Janetta or me throwing out a thought or an observation wasn't working. My tongue was tied. I was searching my brain for where to start.

Janetta picked a handful of pecans from the bowl and set them in front of her. I took a long swallow of my Dr Pepper and waited for the familiar slow burn in my throat. In spite of my sister's slow, deliberate movements, I was more than aware that patience was not one of her virtues.

"OK, this is it," I started, taking a deep breath. "They offered me a job at the White House today."

"What? Who's 'they'?"

"The guy who will be the Media Affairs director at the White House, Jeff Eller. We talked today, and he wants my answer on Monday. If I say yes, I'll need to leave in about a week for Washington, D.C."

I spat all of this out without breathing. The words sounded strange in my own ears. Was I actually talking about me . . . picking up and leaving Arkansas? Moving thousands of miles away from home, from Varner Road, from Daddy? Could the experience possibly be worth all of this?

Janetta slowly, deliberately removed the meat of the pecans from their shells. She chewed slower and slower. My eyes settled on the rusted silver nutcracker she used. I'd accidentally brought the antiquated thing home from one of my Sunday visits to Dad's. That must have been five years ago. I wondered why I'd never returned it. Janetta gingerly set the nuts and the tool down on a paper towel.

"OK, Janis, I know I must have heard you wrong . . ."

My sister's quiet voice belied what I knew was coming. I was listening, trying to conjure up an answer. Another part of my brain was remembering how, when we were younger and my sister visited us from California, I wanted so much to grow up and be just like her. I'd still called her "Dottie," and she'd called me "Faye," our childhood nicknames. I couldn't remember when we'd evolved into proper names. Did that say anything about us, about the difference in our relationship now?

"You are sitting here telling me that this Jeff . . ."

"Jeff Eller," I offered.

"Whoever. You're telling me this person offered you a position in the White House; and you're 'thinking about it,' as if there actually is more than one answer."

Janetta's slight smile was one of incredulity. She was looking down at her hands and slowly shaking her head, again, tousling her thick head of hair. This wasn't good. I swallowed as she began to laugh, low, the way she did when she couldn't believe her ears.

"You've got to be out of your mind to think twice about this, girl."

"Janetta . . . I really need you to help me think this through," I whined. She ignored the age-old antic of mine.

"Why . . . why are we even having this discussion, Janis? As if you can possibly turn down an opportunity like this! There are people who would sell their only child to work in the White House.

"All we need to be talking about, Janis, is the logistics of how you'll get everything done that has to be done within the next week . . . here and at the newspaper. You need to decide who you're going to leave in charge at the newspaper, temporarily; and later, you'll have to put someone permanently in charge."

I sat with my mouth open, unbelieving, shaking my own head now. It simply wasn't that easy, not nearly so settled, as far as I was concerned. But this was Janetta—forcing me to remove the emotional riff-raff I was crowding things with. She would make me look at this through a prism of pure logic and common sense. Janetta was the pragmatic one. Though it often hurt, I admired the way she scraped away the bull and bared the ugly truths.

My parents had called Janetta stubborn and contrary. "That Dottie!" they'd say, exasperated for the millionth time. As an adult, my sister's personality was better defined as "kick ass and take no prisoners." She simply knew better how to orchestrate her life than other people did.

She had left home in the middle of her second year of college after marrying a local boy, a young soldier, whom neither of my parents approved as husband material. If Janetta hesitated because of their disapproval, they never knew it. She had left college and home to move to California with the soldier. For a time, they'd made a good life for themselves.

During her childhood, Janetta had been pretty and smart, but a bit chubbier than the rest of the Kearney girls. She hadn't been in California five years before Mama came back from a summer vacation announcing that Janetta was now skinny. We didn't have access to cameras, at the time, but we were all anxious to see what this new Janetta was like.

We got that opportunity later that year when Dottie came to visit. My older sister had transformed herself from a pretty, chubby girl to a svelte beauty. My first thought was that she'd made herself into Judy Pace, the beautiful black actress from "Peyton Place," the 1960s nighttime TV soap opera. But, in fact, it was Janetta, who was even prettier, just thinner.

It was the late '60s, when most women were discovering the pill, free love and the easiest way to burn bras. Women were being told they deserved more out of life, and they were demanding just that. Janetta was way ahead of the curve. She was already getting more out of life. She was completing both her undergraduate and law degrees while steadily climbing the management ladder at Hughes Aircraft Company in Los Angeles.

———

"Whoa . . . hold up, Janetta. Seriously, I have to decide whether it even makes sense for me to disrupt my life at this point? I'm almost 40 years old. My son just left home to get into college. We're doing OK with the newspaper right now—after it aged me 20 years."

We both laughed some, but I knew there was more than a little truth in it.

"But, seriously, I'd be leaving my family, my friends . . . everything I know here in Arkansas."

Janetta's look told me she thought I was being pathetic.

"Janis, don't even think about weaseling out of this! You're scared, that's the bottom line. And that's OK. But what is it we ever do—that's worth anything—that doesn't scare the crap out of us?"

I stared at my sister, and let out a long, loud sigh.

"Janetta, I'm simply not sure this makes sense for me right now. The timing is all off . . ."

As Janetta waved her beautifully manicured hands in the air, I looked down at my own chubby little-girl hands, with no nails to speak of and certainly no manicure. I had my mother's hands. As I thought this, I wondered what Ethel Kearney would think of all of this.

"The timing doesn't have a darn thing to do with it, Janis. You're making up excuses. The paper will be here when you get back. And, if you want me to, I'll help to make sure everything continues as you want it to.

Whatever you need me to do to help you make this decision, I'll do it."

That was my crafty sister, taking away all my excuses. I was wondering what in the world would I have done at this moment, if my sister wasn't here with me. Her sudden decision to move back to Arkansas from Hawaii a few months ago had been a pleasant surprise. I didn't ask many questions, and she didn't offer many explanations. But that wasn't unusual for the Kearney siblings' philosophy about others' business: "If you want me to know, you'll tell me."

No matter what, I was grateful to have my sister with me at this critical time in my life.

After our hugs and greetings at Little Rock's airport that summer, I told her I hoped she'd stay as long as she wanted, knowing full well that my independent sister wouldn't stay any longer than she absolutely had to.

Janetta had been so much more than a sister for most of my life. She had mentored me during my early adult years and was one of a few people who knew my most private of problems and errors in judgment.

"Janetta, seriously, D.K. will be leaving for college in a few weeks," I'd explained, on our way from the airport. "This house will be too much for just me."

It wasn't just that. I was happy to finally be able to reciprocate her years of kindness. I'd lived in the split-level, wood-frame home on 2217 Vancouver Drive for most of my son's childhood. It was the site of Darryl's and my young love, and our faltering marriage. For the last two years, I'd worked hard to become comfortable with my new existence as a single mother and small business owner.

In many ways, Janetta's life experiences hadn't been much different from mine, and it was heartwarming to sit most evenings commiserating about it all. Except now, it looked as if the opportunity might be snatched away.

As we sat quietly, except for the sound of pecan shells cracking and falling onto the glass table, I wondered if Janetta was right. Was I deceiving myself? Was there something more than my desire to hold on to my home, my friends and my family?

"Tell me, Janetta, would it be so easy for you to just walk away from everything you've always known . . . the things that mean most in your life? What if this was your decision to make?"

"Janis, think about it . . . how many times have I done just that? If I said it should be easy, I'm sorry. I was wrong. I just think there's only one possible answer. But you should just sleep on it. I think you'll make the right decision in the morning."

I nodded slowly, suddenly more exhausted than I'd been in all those months working on the campaign. "That's the best idea I've heard tonight," I joked.

The thoughtful look in Janetta's eyes as she sipped on her tea alerted me that my sister wasn't quite ready to relinquish the fight.

"Yeah, you really should get some rest. I'll see you in the morning . . . but I do think you ought to start thinking about how you'll explain this to Daddy when you tell him."

A new wave of pain and exhaustion came over me as I moved toward the stairway.

"Janis, you need to have your mind made up before you talk to Daddy. It's not his decision, it's yours. Don't use him to help you decide something you'll regret for the rest of your life."

I realized that I was looking for someone else to make my decision for me. I needed to hear someone say this was a crazy idea. I was almost 40 years old, and the only life I'd ever really wanted was falling into place right here in Little Rock.

That's what I hoped my sister would say because I wasn't brave enough to tell myself. It didn't happen quite that way. Janetta wasn't as sympathetic with my pathetic reasoning as I hoped she'd be. She questioned my real reason for my hesitation—fear, loss of what I felt comfortable with, disappointing Daddy?

"You're right. Sunday is the only time I'll have to talk to him . . . whatever my decision is. Good night."

I slowly made my way up the stairway and to my bedroom, still wrestling with the thoughts that would probably rob me of my beloved good night's sleep. Janetta's mention of Daddy was her ace in the hole—how she'd force me to make a decision. I had successfully ignored that giant elephant, until now.

I finally fell asleep that night with questions still scrambled in my brain. I was afraid that if I had to make this decision all alone, it would be the wrong decision. And it was too important to get it wrong.

Of course, Bob, who was already working in the D.C. transition office, wanted me to pack up and get on the plane as soon as I could. He didn't accept my argument that I shouldn't change my life so abruptly. This opportunity, in his mind, was more than enough to merit an abrupt change in my life.

Since Mama's death from cancer in 1982, I'd forged a new bond with my father, whom I'd always loved, but had never enjoyed the same deep relationship as I had with Mama. My new relationship with Daddy was a memorial to Mama, built on our shared loss and his need for continuity in his life. We both needed to continue life as close as possible to the one we'd had when Mama was with us.

Now 10 years later, I was pretty much Daddy's go-to person. He'd become accustomed to a daughter who was always there. He expected the weekend visits, regular phone calls and the guest room in our home when he opted to visit. I admittedly needed that connection to a parent, too. Part of my fear was that my leaving would create a vacuum in my life, as well as his; that it might even erase the bond we'd forged almost 10 years earlier.

I realized just how much change such a decision would entail. It would mean no more Sunday drives to Varner Road. Those drives had been so important to my life. The only change in that ritual for 10 years was my son's decision that he was getting a little old for the weekend visits. He had other interests, and they didn't necessarily include spending Sunday afternoons in the country with his mother and grandfather. But even that hadn't curtailed my weekend trips to Varner Road.

It was times like these that the 90-mile drive from Little Rock to Gould was most useful, most cathartic.

Ninety minutes was plenty of time to mull over all the things going on inside my head, but I wasn't sure it was enough time to come to a resounding resolution.

The drive gave me time to revisit so much in my life, including Jo Ann and our relationship. This was old ground that I'd revisited so many times since her death. Like Janetta, Jo Ann could always separate the bottom line from the BS a lot better than I could. I imagined what she might say as I wrestled with the pros and cons of leaving Arkansas for Washington.

My younger sister had always been able to peek behind my veneer, read my mind better than anyone I knew. She had always shoved my face in the truth when I tried to look away. I had the strange feeling that Jo Ann was sitting somewhere half smiling, waiting to see how I handled this dilemma.

My 1963 religious conversion was the one thing that reminded me most of just how much influence my younger sister held over me. Truthfully, my obsessive need to please likely had just as much to do with my decision to join the mourners' bench at the age of 9—just one month shy of my 10th birthday. My saved soul wasn't so much what I yearned for, as it was what I believed my parents wanted for me—especially since Jo Ann "got her religion" the year before.

And because I have always remembered the big things in my life in juxtaposition with even larger things happening in the world, I know that my religious conversion took place just three months before the assassination of President Kennedy.

It was actually my second time around on Rankin Chapel's mourners' bench—that front and center wooden bench where we, the "unsaved," sat through nights of emotional preaching until our will, or our religious barriers, gave way. Revivals were the climax of the year, the real purpose of churches put in action—pulling souls from the jaws of hell.

Not only did the preachers toss your emotions from one end of the church aisles to the other, but church members known to cause the most violent of shouting, knelt just feet from us, praying loudly, fervently, and sometimes in other tongues—all for your conversion from sinner to saint.

Well, Jo Ann had been converted, then baptized the year before—one cause for my resentment in the knowledge that my younger sister was always one step ahead of me.

That year I'd convinced myself that God simply had his hands full with all his other converts. I was sorely tempted to force God's hand, though, when Jo Ann got up, crying and shaking and claiming that God had called her from the mourners' bench.

The next year I was determined that, at almost 10 years old, God had to be ready for my soul. For five nights straight I sat on that hard, wooden bench with the rest of the children—some near my age, some even younger—letting the tears roll down my face, waiting for God to move me to repent and give up my sinful soul.

Finally, finally, on the last night of revival, the message I'd been waiting for had arrived. It was a typically hot and muggy August night; and when I rose from the mourners' bench, sweat trickled down my face onto my clothing. The tears, I'm almost convinced, were genuine. For certain, the trembling was. I can't truthfully say whether my happiness—or relief—was more about joining Jo Ann's league or about joining God's.

I turned, shivering and crying as I searched for Mama's face. I found it amid the other church mothers and sisters who were swaying and moaning in their seats, all grateful for another soul for Jesus. I saw the small smile of victory on my mother's soft face.

When the pastor walked down from the pulpit, a smile of accomplishment was painted across his face. I was ready—more than ready—to declare myself saved. When he asked if I had anything to say, I blurted out what I'd heard Jo Ann say. "I'm saved . . . thank God, I'm saved!"

As I sobbed and wiped tears from my face, I glimpsed Mama sitting on the second row of pews, nodding and dabbing her eyes with a white handkerchief. Strangely, the women were all silently congratulating her, smiling at her, fanning her and patting her back as if to say, "finally, finally." Each seemed to look over at me at the same time, nodding. I imagined their thoughts, "You done good, girl. You made your mama proud." I imagine, in reality, they were even happier that my late conversion would allow them to go home before midnight.

"Another soul for God's kingdom, Church!" the diminutive minister's deep voice resonated throughout the small church. "Ain't God good?"

Reverend C.L. Washington was a small man with a large man's voice; a beautiful voice that could easily mesmerize a little girl sitting on the mourners' bench.

That night, he beckoned me with his outstretched hand, and I noticed even through my trembling and tears that his hand wasn't much larger than my own small hand. I grasped it and moved closer until I was standing very near the small minister.

"Turn, Dear, and face the church," he said sweetly.

I turned and saw what felt like thousands of eyes staring back at me. Reverend Washington smiled and clasped my shoulder as if I was his child. And though I was not quite 10 years old and one year short of getting my first period, Reverend Washington declared to the church and the world that I was "plenty old enough for God."

Unlike funerals, most rural, black churches hurried baptisms along as if they were afraid the new converts would back slide before they were fully ordained saints.

Our baptism was set for the next Sunday at Reverend Washington's church "in town". First Baptist Church was the largest black church in Gould, a stark contrast to small, rural Rankin Chapel, which nearly burst at the seams if more than 200 people crowded inside.

I was sure that First Baptist Church was for the rich black people in town, while Rankin Chapel was for the poor, hardworking families like ours.

Members of First Baptist Church included our schoolteachers and parents of the teachers' pets—the well-dressed, smart students. Many of the adults owned impressive land acreage or their own small businesses.

First Baptist was a large and imposing white building that took up a full corner lot. It sat just blocks off U.S. Highway 65, but its steeple could be seen clear across the tracks.

Inside, the aisles were wide, the floor was carpeted, and there were endless rows of pews. Rumor had it that the church had seated as many as a thousand people during one service. The pastor's pulpit was something to behold. It reminded my 10-year-old sensibilities of a royal throne. The minister's seat was in the center of the stage that served as a foundation for the pulpit. It was raised higher than the other seating.

The floor behind the pulpit opened to the baptismal pool, and above the pool was a breath-taking portrait of Jesus and his disciples. In the back of the church, directly behind the pulpit and baptismal pool, were a fully operational kitchen and dining room, a daycare for children threatening to interrupt Reverend Washington's Sunday services, and separate inside bathrooms for men and women.

On baptismal day, I sat in the back seat of our station wagon with my younger siblings and gloated. Like Mama and Daddy and some of my older siblings, I was saved. I was one of 10 children chosen by God for baptism that year, along with a couple of adults who had "back slid" for years and finally got around to returning to the flock. One or two were strangers who must have had to leave their homes to find God—away from the people who knew them best.

We all felt especially lucky to be baptized in the church pool at this city church with its ceiling fans and warm water. Most of my older siblings had had to shiver through their baptisms in one of the muddy bayous outside town.

Later in life, I would have to think hard to remember what was real and what wasn't about that day. Most memorable is the illuminating whiteness of the day. I remember that we all—boys, girls, men and women—dressed in long, white gowns and caps that the church ushers had made for us.

Yet, in all my pure surroundings and in spite of my happiness about "finding God," I hadn't been able to rid myself of a small, hard pebble in my stomach that day—nagging questions I couldn't shut out. Questions about the God I had committed my life to and "the new me" I would be stuck with for the rest of my life.

I saw in the other children's eyes how serious a thing this was. Their eyes were big and round and accepting of this new religious journey. Their jaws were set with determination. There seemed to be no questions rattling around in their heads or hard pebbles in their stomachs. I envied them.

The grown folks looked happily over at us, singing as we awaited our immersion. I swallowed my uneasiness. Reverend Washington had forewarned us all that this oath wasn't something to take lightly . . . or, in my mama's stern words, "You don't go playin' with God!" Moments before I was dipped into the lukewarm water, I fervently prayed to my new God to make sure I was making the right decision.

I truly tried to erase the thoughts about what I was giving up for this new religion—the childhood that would be no more. No more watching my brothers swim naked in the bayou behind the house. No more playing tricks on the cats by feeding them milk, then pulling the washtub down on their heads. Not even would I be able to step on my classmates change when it fell and pretend I was helping to look for it, until they left.

The walk to the baptismal pool seemed as long as one of Daddy's cotton rows. Yet, I couldn't stop ticking off the things I had to say goodbye to—no more playing foolish games with my siblings 'til the middle of the night or roughhousing it with the neighbors' children that sometimes ended in fights and tears. I couldn't pick fights with my younger brothers who didn't know yet that they could whip me senseless . . . if only they'd known. And no more swiping quarters from Mama's purse when I was too embarrassed to go on field trips without one red cent.

I clicked my mind shut and followed the slow line of white gowns that made their way down into the pool. I half smiled, just mildly relieved, to see that Daddy and Deacon Parks—a First Baptist deacon—would escort us up to Reverend Washington.

My father was thin, but strong; and Deacon Parks was stocky and strong. They each held one of my elbows as I half walked, half paddled the few feet through the waist-high water. They stood grasping my elbows, assuring that I wouldn't float away, as Reverend Washington offered his scared and shivering lamb up to God.

I know now that my mind still wasn't where it was supposed to be. I noticed, without any effort, that the water was clear up to the tiny reverend's chest. I was sure he must have worn platform shoes in our pulpit because at that moment he was less than an inch taller than me.

The short, dark minister wore thick, round eyeglasses and held his large, black Bible up out of the water. An image of the cartoon character, Mr. Magoo, passed fleetingly through my mind, but I hurriedly pushed it away. Reverend Washington's clearing his throat helped me to clear the foolishness from my mind.

As the minister prepared to introduce this newly cleansed child of God to the congregation, he smiled and peered into my eyes—no, beyond my eyes—as if he could read my mind and heart. I desperately tried to hide any unseemly thoughts or questions from his sight.

"Church, this is Sister Janis Kearney." The small man had a deep, resonating voice that must have served him well in his chosen career of saving souls. Most of his statement went right past me, though. I was fighting to control my trembling in the lukewarm water.

I did manage to affirm my commitment to God. I wondered, though, why he hadn't called me "Faye." Only my classmates knew me as Janis because that's what my teachers called me. To my friends out on Varner Road and my family, I was Faye, and I feared that because of this simple oversight, they might not know I was giving my soul to God.

Reverend Washington suddenly closed his eyes, pulling the Bible closer to his chest. It was a baleful prayer he sent up to God on my behalf. "With the power vested in me, I baptize you, Janis Kearney, in the name of the Father, the name of the Son, and the name of the Holy Ghost. Aaamen!"

Reverend Washington, with the assistance of my father and Deacon Parks, gently pulled me backward and down into the water—not for a long time, but long enough for me to panic. In that brief moment, I imagined myself drowning with my father watching. Just seconds later, however, they were straightening me, standing me up on my feet. I was disoriented, shivering and sopping wet.

Through my water-pained eyes, I saw Reverend Washington's beaming face, his round eyes twinkling through the round lenses. A smile spread clear across his wide mouth as if I was his disciple, not God's.

I was the last of the converted 10 to be baptized that day. The last, in a line of newly cleansed, and the last to shower and dress for the church service that immediately followed the baptism.

All dried and dressed in our white clothing, we sat on display at the front of the church as Reverend Washington delivered a thunderous sermon of gratitude for his flock. I imagined, given our newly cleansed souls, there was nothing to distinguish us from each other any more. We were all now God's children—all shrouded in the white that symbolized purity and all newly baptized, a symbol of the washing away of earthly sins.

And I did feel cleaner, almost weightless, as if I could fly away into the heavens at that moment. This was an awesome feeling of being not me, but something beyond, something better.

That feeling lingered for weeks, maybe months, until one day I realized it was gone. I believed I was saved, but the wonderful pure feeling was no longer with me each day. My parents had made it clear that I'd have to work to hold on to that elusive thing called sainthood, yet I'd not imagined it could disappear so quickly, so completely.

I found a way to mention the painful loss to Jo Ann, in hopes that she would tell me what she did to recapture hers. The wise girl's smile told me everything. She knew. She'd always know.

I was nearing Varner Road. If I swerved right, the road would take me straight to the infamous Cummins Prison farm. I was on my way home and remembering Jo Ann's frequent impatience with me—the less wise, though older sister. I knew she'd likely say I had become too comfortable, too secure in my life. She would look into my eyes and see the fear of change and of losing the new bond with Daddy and maybe even learning I wasn't indispensable after all.

Surely, anyone would understand how I felt. Going to Washington was entering a new world, a place where I knew few people and few people knew me. Life is sometimes scary, I could hear Jo Ann say. Get on with it.

I imagined my sister taking her leave before we arrived at the place where we grew up. Now it was up to me. Driving the five miles down Varner Road allowed me time to remember the neighbors who had been a part of my life during my growing-up years.

I thought about our unique surrogate mother, Mrs. Oldie Lee Land; Mrs. Mary Henderson, who had pressed and curled the Kearney girls hair for decades for as little as 25 cents and never more than a dollar; the widows Mary Jackson and her daughter Verline, both schoolteachers, who had kept half a dozen rabid dogs that scared us senseless as we walked from our home to Mrs. Henderson's for our Saturday night press and curl.

We wondered whether the women knew the dogs were as dangerous as they were.

Then there was the only other man I'd seen who was as tall as Mr. Henry Land—our white neighbor Fred Lack, who owned the cotton field directly across from our house. Even though they were our second-closest neighbors, it never really crossed my mind that in all the years we chopped the Lacks' cotton, there was seldom one word to pass between us.

I was minutes from home, rounding the curve that was less than a mile from Daddy's home. His small house had been painted a greenish blue some years ago because Daddy found the white too boring. The small plot of land was a thing of pride for my parents when they moved off the leased land onto the two acres off Varner Road.

Daddy had built the eight-room house in 1962 with some help from neighbors. The land, the house Daddy built, and the trees he'd planted to please Mama were all so inextricably tied to James Kearney's existence and to mine.

During those early months of newspaper ownership, I'd somehow forgotten what this place, this visit, meant to me. I had been overwhelmed with getting things right at the paper, and because of that, my bond with Daddy had loosened for a time. I was sure now that no irrevocable damage was done. Daddy understood. The weekly visits resumed as soon as I could raise my head above water and I was sure I wouldn't bring my stresses down with me.

Ever since Mama's passing, I'd encouraged Daddy to spend more weekends in Little Rock with D.K.

and me—even if I had to duck out sometimes for work. Not that Daddy needed me or D.K. to entertain him; he would always be fine all by himself as long as there was a newspaper, a book or a television with sports and game shows. I'd learned just how much I treasured this bond—his visits to Little Rock and my Sunday visits to Varner Road. And now I had resolved to give them up, for a time at least.

As always, Daddy had been watching for my car. He was standing in his yard when I drove up. I reached to turn off the ignition and felt a gentle flutter, as if small parts of my heart might be breaking. As I resolved what I was here to tell my father, I remembered Janetta's warning. She was right. I'd have to stick to my decision no matter what.

Though it was in the middle of winter, Daddy's yard was adorned with colorful perennials he and Mama had planted so many years ago. Daddy planted the flowers in remembrance of both his wife and his own mother who had loved gardening more than anything.

Gratefully, I have no memory of the relationship between my mother and grandmother, but from all accounts, these two women had no love for each other. My grandmother lived in our home for several years, and I can imagine those were likely some of my mother's unhappiest years.

I was home. I smiled through the window, stepped out and slammed the car door shut before walking over to hug Daddy. I could already hear his football game blasting through the door and out into the yard.

"You're looking great, Daddy. How was church?" We walked into the house, and I continued through the living room to the television set to turn the volume down.

"Daddy, you are ruining your hearing."

"I'm glad to see you made it here OK."

He smiled, heading for his straight-back chair. This was now the only chair Daddy felt comfortable sitting in. I reminded myself, as I always did, that my father was 89 years old. He had never looked his age, and at 89 he was independent and moved with as much pep as a man 30 years his junior.

"Church service was fine ... just too long as usual. We had a pretty good crowd, though, almost 50 people. That new preacher is already keeping us too long. I was starving by the time I got here. I already ate a little snack, so I won't be hungry enough for dinner for a little while. I took some pork chops down from the freezer. By the time they thaw, I'll be hungry again. I think I got a taste for some mashed potatoes, too. I hadn't had any in a while."

Daddy was channel surfing, secure that his meal would be taken care of. I smiled to myself, muttering: "spoiled, spoiled, spoiled."

"Did you say something, Faye?" he asked, as he leaned forward, peering at the grainy television screen.

"So, you guys already got yourselves another preacher, and he's turned out to be just as long-winded, huh?" I was rifling through the stack of mail Daddy deposited on one of his living room tables. There were always letters addressed to one of his children from the alumni offices of the various colleges and universities.

"You'd think these people would have something better to spend their 32 cents on . . . or at least find your children's correct addresses by now." I shook my head. There were birthday cards and Christmas cards spanning months.

"They've been sending these letters for the last 30 years," Daddy said. "I use to write 'wrong address' on 'em and send 'em back. That never worked."

"You sure you can wait to eat dinner, Daddy? I can go on and get started."

Daddy shook his head, already settled back in his chair, ready to enjoy the football game.

"No, I can wait. How's Janetta doing? She OK?"

"She's fine. She told me to make sure I tell you 'Hi.' "

He nodded and offered a half smile. "She started working, yet?"

"Daddy, she just got here. Give her time to catch her breath. She'll find a job in plenty of time. You know she's got more experience than all of us put together."

I walked through the door to the narrow hallway that separated the living room from the sleeping area. I stared for a time at the old, wooden picture frame hanging across from the two guest beds. It was crowded with images of Kearney children. Daddy had made the frame from stove wood he'd cut and stacked outdoors one fall. Some of the instant Kodak images had long ago faded and were identifiable only to us, and only because we were there when the photos were taken.

I peered at a '60s shot of myself. I was still amazed to see the girl with the older-than-her-years pose. I was wearing a pair of the "in" stretch pants and a familiar T-shirt. My younger brothers Jerome and Jude stood grinning on each side of me.

In the center of the collage was a clear photo of a young, beautiful woman sitting on a bench with her hands clasped in her lap and her legs crossed at the ankles. The faint smile said so much and yet so little. In spite of the reality of her life as a sharecropper's wife, my mother's proud bearing had changed little during her 64 years.

I wondered whether she would be disappointed I was about to leave Arkansas. Would she view my decision as that of an uncaring daughter abandoning an aging father? I imagined her pursing her lips, insinuating I was being foolish and giving up too much for too little in return.

Ethel Kearney had accepted her role as a caretaker to her husband. For 45 years, she attended to the most menial of his needs . . . from cutting his hair to laying out his underwear. She was an amazing study in contrasts—a woman who was as fiercely independent as she was unabashedly traditional. She wasn't the least bit ashamed to place her husband and children above everything else in her life.

I'd only been Daddy's weekend caregiver for the last 10 years and was more than willing to continue that role as long as he needed me. Unlike Mama, though, I was no traditionalist. While I certainly valued marriage, I had other missions in life as well.

Over the years, I had depended on my mother's wise counsel and support. She was conservative and prudent, a woman who was more ears than mouth—only giving advice when her children demanded it . . . not just because we merely asked.

It had always been useless to try and get Mama to take our sides when it came to marital problems. She never would. She would sit with that half smile of hers, sometimes looking into your eyes, sometimes busying herself with something else, as she listened. She comforted and even empathized, but she refused to tell you what you should do.

Now as I was about to make this daunting change in my life, I needed Mama more than I ever had. Even if she didn't agree with my decision to go, I wanted to see that look in her eyes that said she wasn't a bit surprised. I needed to hear her say she was proud of me.

⸻

I heard Daddy's familiar, light Sunday evening snoring. I walked out his back door, enjoying the pleasant cool of the winter day. Daddy's wayward dogs slept under this year's amazingly fertile pecan trees. This was a far more difficult goodbye than the one I'd made in leaving for college, or even when I'd married Darryl in 1973. Saying goodbye to this place that had grounded and nurtured me transported me back to when I was a 17-year-old going away to college.

It was time. Daddy should be eating soon. The three dogs stirred from their slumber and lazily checked me out, sniffing the space around for assurance they were safe. They were lousy watchdogs, but they were good company to Daddy. They were also cheap boarders—satisfied with Daddy's morning and evening feedings.

I prayed that before I left, Daddy would give me his blessings. I needed to know that I had been a blessing to him since Mama had left us. Jo Ann had me pegged right. I would always need my parents' approval, those mostly unspoken, but meaningful pats on the head, that told me "I did good."

I tiptoed past Daddy, who was still snoring, and washed my hands in the tiny bathroom. I returned to the kitchen to prepare our dinner of fried pork chops, gravy, mashed potatoes and turnip greens. It was a typical dinner on Varner Road and a typical January Sunday, except it wasn't.

Daddy cleared his throat to let me know he was awake. His slow steps to the television set alerted me that he was ready to watch the rest of the football game.

"Did you have a good sleep, Daddy?" I remembered just as the words were uttered that James Kearney never admitted to sleeping during the day.

"Oh, I just closed my eyes for a while. I was still listening to the football game."

I hurriedly plopped the white potatoes in the boiling water and pulled Daddy's cooked turnip greens from the refrigerator to warm up.

"You still have some good-looking greens out there."

Daddy grunted, his eyes still glued to the muscle-bound boy running down the field with the football clutched under his arm.

I rinsed, then seasoned and floured the hefty pork chops before settling them down into the half-inch of boiling vegetable oil. The aroma quickly filled the house, reminding me of days past when Mama moved around in her kitchen preparing dinner, and I was just her helper.

I couldn't believe it had been so many years ago. I missed those days as if they were last week. I checked the turnip greens Daddy had cooked before leaving for church this morning. I shook my head at the small piece of salt pork he insisted on using for seasoning. I knew it was futile to try and control my 89-year-old father's fat or sugar intake. His arteries were probably less clogged than mine.

"Daddy, can we talk about something before dinner?" I wanted to get past the hard part of this visit. I didn't want to discuss moving away to Washington as I faced my elderly father at dinner. I was stirring the greens far too long.

Daddy turned from the television screen, looking quizzically over at me. I had interrupted his most important pastime of the day.

"Yeah, Faye, what is it?"

"Well, I wanted to talk to you about something that came up suddenly this past week. You already know that I'm still working in Governor Clinton's transition office. I had planned to go back to the newspaper in a few weeks..."

"Yeah, you told me. You're not going back to the newspaper now? What's happened?"

"Well... I was. But now... I was asked if I wanted to go to the White House to work for the president."

Daddy's unbelieving eyes stayed on me for a moment before he looked away to see what the spectators were cheering about. Then he'd done a most amazing thing, one for the books. My daddy clicked the television off, and the football game wasn't even at halftime.

A Chapter in An Unfinished Life (1993)

"I see. When did they ask you? When do they want you to go? What will happen to the newspaper?"

"They asked me to tell them tomorrow when I get back to the office. But I really wanted to talk to you first, before I talked to them . . . before I gave them my answer."

"Humph . . . that's something. I hadn't thought about you going up there. I mean, I was really happy Bill Clinton won, but . . . I hadn't thought about you going up there when he goes."

"I know, and I really hadn't even thought about it, either. But it just came up. And, the truth is, it would be a once-in-a-lifetime opportunity. There aren't many people who get this kind of opportunity." I knew Dad's interest would be piqued by the historical value of such a thing.

"Yeah, that's true. It would be. Well . . . " This was all the response I'd get right now.

"Let's eat dinner, Daddy. We'll talk about it some more after we eat." Of course, he didn't know how to respond. I wasn't even sure! We were quiet for a long time.

"You still like loads of butter in your mashed potatoes, Daddy?"

"Yeah, yeah, I do. It's the only way I'll eat them."

"Rather than Cokes, you want me to fix some lemonade?"

"Yeah, yeah, that sounds fine. Your mama used to like to fix lemonade."

"Daddy, I'm sorry I brought this up before dinner. We won't talk about it anymore until we eat, OK?"

"Oh, that's fine. I'm just surprised, hadn't thought about it. I guess I just hate to think about you being so far away. You hear so many terrible things about that place, about the crime and all."

Daddy had remained eternally young. But today as we talked, the words, the thought of my leaving had magically revealed that he was aging. He sat quiet, staring at the screen. But I was sure his mind was not on the boys playing football. He looked over at me, then back at the television.

"You oughta go, Faye. I'm just an old, selfish father thinking about how I'll miss having you here. You can't turn down a chance to do something like this. I'll be fine . . . it'll just take me a while to get used to not having you here."

I wiped the tears away before they slid down my cheeks and into the buttery mashed potatoes. At that moment, I didn't want to go away to Washington or to the White House or anywhere farther than the 90 miles from Varner Road.

"Would you really be all right if I went, Daddy? You have to be honest. Do you think you'll be OK?"

He nodded, frowning, not sure. "Yeah, I'll be fine. Mary comes down and checks on me most weeks. I'm just being a jealous old man, that's all."

Mary, yes, I'd forgotten about Daddy's female friend. I was ashamed to admit that her being there to spend time with him made me feel a lot better.

As I finished cooking and set the table, the afternoon was almost the same as it always was. The tears had disappeared. Again, I realized the comforting thought that Mary Witherspoon was in my father's life. Just a few years ago, the "good Christian woman," as Daddy had described her, had become a regular staple in Daddy's life. He began driving the 10 miles to Dumas to visit her, and sometimes he even drove her to his home on Varner Road.

Watching Daddy forge a relationship with a woman besides our mother had been hard for most of us, initially. It was hardest, though, for his sons. They seemed unable to imagine any woman other than Mama being a part of Daddy's life. It would take some time.

Nothing convinced me that Daddy needed someone in his life more than my decision to leave. He needed companionship the same as his children, and I believed the 80-year-old widow was exactly what Daddy needed. They were company for each other and, I thought selfishly, she would distract him from remembering what and who wasn't there. She would help dull his missing my visits, my weekly companionship.

Daddy sat at the head of the table, as he always did. I ate and looked out over the yard and beyond, into the woods. Daddy was quiet, but his appetite seemed unaffected by our discussion.

"Everything's good, Faye. The potatoes are just like I like them."

"Thanks, Daddy. I'm glad you like them."

After dinner, I sent Daddy back to his football game while I cleaned the dishes and straightened the kitchen. My going to Washington had settled in the room, but the rough edges of it had softened some. Finally, I sat on the sofa near Daddy's chair.

"Daddy, what if I promise to visit every chance I get?"

"How often you think you can come?"

"Maybe once every other month ... once I get there and get settled in. I already have leads on a house. A television cameraman and his sister will lease their parents' home to me, if I decide to go."

Daddy nodded. "That's good. The prices up there a lot higher, I know. I don't know how people live in places like that."

Our Sunday evenings had always been times for calm and simple enjoyment of sharing our space. I finally sat, joining Daddy in watching the cloudiness of the television screen and listening to the jarring, overexcited voices of the sportscasters. I silently thanked God that the hardest part of my visit was behind me.

As I prepared to leave, the sun was almost behind the woods, seemingly dipping into the bayou that sat behind our home. Dusk had always been my favorite time of day on Varner Road. As a child, my dreams often took flight just as this otherworldly, ephemeral beauty of the rural world came alive.

As I began my drive back to Little Rock, Daddy stood at the old, rusting mailbox waving and smiling bravely. I tooted my horn, yelling desperately, "I love you, Daddy!" Still waving, still smiling, he'd yelled back, "I love you, too." I'd received his blessings. Yet, I was hurting; my heart was breaking. Was an opportunity of a lifetime really worth so much?

I watched in my rearview mirror as Daddy grew smaller and smaller while still standing at the old mailbox. I smiled sadly to myself, as I thought of the scenes in the old, black-and-white movies where the woman drives away in tears. But, unable to go on, she suddenly stops the car and rushes back, her face streaked with tears, to say a last emotional goodbye.

I wouldn't stop the car, risk changing my mind. The decision had been too difficult, too painful. I turned away from the rearview mirror, imagining Daddy growing older. I wished for more resolve to erase the small beads of doubt. This journey was necessary, predestined. Wasn't that what Daddy had taught us, about dreams, about impossibilities, about preparing ourselves for miracles?

Yet, I was giving up so much ... would miss so much about our Sundays on Varner Road; the visits to Sunday school, where Daddy was still superintendent after more than 50 years; and the warm and friendly hugs from those who remembered me as "Faye" growing up there. I would miss hearing their comments: "My goodness, if you aren't the spittin' image of Miss Ethel!"

I'd miss the cool, spicy fragrance of Aqua Velva aftershave that Daddy had fallen in love with in 1965. His 9-year old son, Jerome, had bought it at Fish's Grocery Store, wrapped it with care and delivered it proudly on Christmas morning. Since then, the smooth, rounded blue bottle had never disappeared from my father's bathroom cabinet.

I'd miss the sweet, buttery aroma of Daddy's homemade yeast rolls that sometimes met me at the door, informing me that Daddy's morning had been one full of reminisces of his life with Mama. Those days ended either in naps in the living room or passionate discussions about politics—no more one-sided lectures once I was old enough to express my own opinions.

It was the 90-minute drive to Route 1, Varner Road, though, that I would miss most. Going home to the place of my past, and where the Kearney family still gathered. Daddy's blessings had been a prerequisite for my journey. Yet, my heart broke to see that his eyes held more than blessings, something sadder than pride. For the first time, I regretted the long drive back to Little Rock that would allow me to remember all that I would miss . . . all that I would lose in this journey to Washington and the White House.

There were other times we shared that had little to do with Sundays, like our jaunts through the state, and even a 27-hour trip to Los Angeles, and a shorter trip to Louisiana where we visited Daddy's brother and his wife in Columbus. There were also the times I served as chauffeur/chaperone as he visited the attractive widow of his once best friend and the odd feeling surrounding those visits as they sat comfortably remembering their pasts.

I would miss our passionate discussions about politics. We'd both been full of all the right answers. Sometimes Daddy would call late in the night to say he'd meant to say one more thing or he'd just remembered one point.

I would never forget the joy of sharing Daddy's first movie in 50 years—seeing his eyes light up as he talked about "Driving Miss Daisy" months after he'd sat in the dark theater with D.K. and me. I'd miss my chance at seeing that kind of joy a second time.

I wished now that I was already home.

By the time I arrived at Highway 65, I felt a little less sad, a little more hopeful. Daddy's blessings were sincere. He was proud of me—his eyes had held both sadness and pride. Maybe there was an ounce of grief still to be contended with, but the pride was real. And it would be fresh in his mind and heart next Sunday. I knew James Kearney well enough to know that when he shared the news at Rankin Chapel—that his daughter was going to the White House—he'd try to temper the fatherly pride. But it would still shine through. And it would be real.

January 16th was my last night as a full-time resident at 2217 Vancouver Drive. The bulging suitcase I'd packed sat on the floor of the living room. I boxed up clothing I'd carry to Washington on my next visit home and bagged up bundles for Goodwill that I'd never fit in again. Yes, I was finally getting rid of the tight-fitting bell-bottoms I hung onto to remind myself of my early college days, the wraparound skirts that didn't quite make it around anymore, the bodysuits that had clearly overstretched their limit, and the sexy miniskirts that really were cute on me—once upon a time.

There were boxes of outdated magazines and books that had lost their backs, once-important papers I'd crushed into drawers to go through later, pictures of people I had no memories of, and lots of just plain useless trash.

I was hoping I'd packed enough clothes to last me at least a month. I also believed I would be able to steal a weekend over the next couple of months to come home and claim my beloved Mitsubishi Galant and the rest of my clothes.

Janetta chose that weekend out of all the rest to travel to Hawaii on business. When I half jokingly accused her of abandoning me during my moment of need, she'd laughed through the phone.

"Girl, please . . . you know I'd be there if I could, but I have to get back to Hawaii to take care of some business."

"Well, I'll call you when I get there and get settled," I'd promised her. I really did understand her predicament.

"Take care of yourself, Janis, and don't worry about anything back here. After this visit, I shouldn't have to travel for a while. I'll keep an eye on the house, and we can discuss what you need me to do for the paper."

Alma, my best friend and my newspaper's accountant for the past couple of years, called to say she was on her way over.

"I know I have to get there before you go to bed with the chickens, like you always do!"

I said I was wide-awake and hoped to have most of the packing done by the time she arrived. After we hung up, though, my exhaustion and drooping were a reality. The telephone roused me. It was D.K. calling to check in on me before I left out for D.C.

"Hey, Mom. I thought you'd be in bed by now. What are you doing up?" I could hear my son's beautiful smile through the phone.

"I'm packing up some stuff and throwing away a bunch. Alma's coming over in a little while to say goodbye. After that, I'll be hitting the sack."

"Are you ready to leave? Are you nervous, excited?"

"All of the above," I said. We laughed. There was a pause.

"Mama, I'm happy for you and excited about you taking the giant step. But I was thinking tonight that I'm not so sure how I feel with you not being there when I come home. In fact, I guess in a little while, we won't really have a home anymore." D.K.'s weak laughter made me know this was something serious with him.

"But we will have a home . . . it'll just be in D.C. You'll come there now."

"I guess so . . . but it won't be the same."

"Are you sorry I'm going, D.K? You can tell me the truth."

"No, really, I'm not. I guess . . . we've really been through a lot of changes over the last few years." I frowned. My son was referring to my change from a normal, doting mom to one obsessed with the newspaper, followed up by a divorce—an even more painful kind of change in our lives.

"I guess it has been a lot. But would it make things better if I stayed here?"

"No, no, I think you should definitely go. It's a once-in-a-lifetime opportunity!"

"Thank you, D.K. That means a lot to me. In fact, hearing you say that is exactly what I needed tonight."

"Aw . . . come on, Mom. Believe me, I'm more than just OK with your going to the White House. I've already started telling everybody on campus about you!"

We both laughed before he apologized for having to go.

"I love you, Mama. Call me when you get to D.C."

"I love you, too, babe. I'll call you as soon as I get there!"

A melancholy smile lingered on my lips as I placed the phone back on the receiver. Though tears stood in my eyes, I was resolute now that I'd made the right decision. Minutes later the doorbell rang, and I wiped my eyes before hurrying downstairs.

Alma stood at the door with a wide smile and a bottle of wine. After I ushered her inside, and through the living room, to my work in progress upstairs, she laughed. "My God! This looks like a war zone!"

"I didn't tell you it would be pretty!"

"It looks like you're all packed and ready to blow this joint."

I shrugged. "I guess there's no turning back at this point, anyway," I joked.

"Nope. Why would you even think of turning back? You're going to this exciting new life. You should be jumping for joy."

"Then why am I having these stomach flutters?" I asked, only half joking.

She laughed, but after a moment offered, "I guess you're right. It's exciting stuff, but I'm not so sure what I'd do in your place. I mean, I'm really happy for you, but I know it would be harder for me. Remember, I have two children still at home." We were quiet for a moment.

" I do hope you'll remember to be careful up there . . . and not be so trusting of any and everybody like you always are."

I frowned and shrugged. "Thanks, Alma, for the show of confidence. I'll make sure I look both ways before crossing the streets, and not walk down dark alleys, and refuse to talk to strangers . . ."

She shook her head, and we both laughed.

"Seriously, though, other than what's on your memo, is there anything else I need to know about or need to monitor while you're gone?"

I shook my head. "Nothing I can think of right now, but if I think of something, I'll call. I'm a little worried about things, but I'll be just a phone call away."

I was confident that my temporary replacement, Patrice Brown, would do a find job, but I asked Alma to help out if Patrice needed it. Janetta had promised she would help, too.

"Don't worry, things will be fine. There won't be anything more going wrong than it was when you were here trying to hold everything together. And on the subject of holding things together, what about Bob?"

We giggled like schoolgirls. It was common knowledge now that Bob had gone to D.C. to work on the transition team and would be joining the Clinton administration, as well. We were together the evening the president-elect had called and asked him to serve.

"Well . . . " I stammered. "I haven't mentioned it to anyone, but we've decided it would be a lot cheaper if we moved in together . . . I mean, since I've already found a house."

Alma rolled her eyes and snickered. "And how long do you think that's going to be a secret, the way gossip flies in this town?"

"I didn't say I was trying to keep it a secret. We just haven't made a public announcement."

It was midnight when Alma gathered her purse and coat and stood up to leave. There had been tears after all. I wondered later that night if I'd ever find a friend like Alma in a place like Washington. After our hugs, tears and goodbyes, I walked through the house, up the stairs and into my son's empty room.

Until that night, D.K had been a "not sure" on my mental list of people supporting my move. He had been one of the first people I'd called, and we'd talked about the move almost every night during the last week.

Though he had been excited, like any college student would be, I was still afraid my son viewed my move as an abandonment of our past. As we'd both agreed, the newspaper and the divorce had changed both our lives. Even with that truth, I was able to mentally place a check mark beside my son's name. D.K.'s support was so important to my peace of mind, as I began this journey.

I closed the blinds, shutting out the slices of light from the outside, turned off the light and walked back into the hallway. I sat for a while on the stairway, taking a moment to say goodbye to my home, my sanctuary for half of my adult life.

I would look deep inside and find an honest answer as to why this journey had to be. I couldn't turn back now. Maybe no one else would understand it, but I knew this journey was as much about honoring my past as it was about my future. The final decision was inextricably tied to the sacrifices my parents had made, about the magic of their dreams and the life lessons they had passed on to us so many years ago.

A Chapter in An Unfinished Life (1993)

Tears, again. In spite of my tentative excitement, there was still the fear. Tomorrow would be the start of another journey, another chapter in my life. I had no crystal ball that predestined how it would all turn out, but the beginning was the first page in a dream that began long ago on Varner Road.

PART IV

SOMETHING TO WRITE HOME ABOUT

(1993–1995)

Janis F. Kearney
The White House
Washington, DC 20016

James Kearney
Varner Road
Gould, AR 71643

January 17, 1993

Hey Daddy,

Sorry it took me this long to write, but I just made it here yesterday, and everything happened so fast. I didn't have time to do much packing, so I wasn't able to bring very much with me. I left just about everything back home, and it's freezing up here.

How have you been?? I miss you, and it was really good talking to you last week. I miss our phone calls, solving the world's problems, deciding which leaders need to be run out of office. I guess we'll both have to change our tunes a bit now. (smile)

How is everyone down that way ... The Calloways, Miss Josephine, and all the folks at church? Tell the Kings I miss them, and I'll call them when I get the chance. Do you still talk to Mrs. King every night? I'm really glad to know you guys keep in touch ... I do wonder sometimes if Mr. King might get a little jealous sometimes (smile). When was the last time the gang was down? I really miss my weekend visits.

I talked to most everyone before leaving, and they were all happy for me, but pretty much stunned that I was actually leaving Arkansas. I tried to tell them that once I got your and D.K.'s blessings, it really wasn't that hard a decision for me.

I feel really lucky that this was D.K.'s first year in college, and I didn't have to worry about uprooting him from school. Dad, I still feel that I'll wake up from a dream one of these mornings and will be back down in Little Rock. Maybe it's all the sleep I'm missing that has me thinking like that. (smile) I do think D.K. is a little excited that his mom is working at the White House. I'm sure it makes for good conversation with his friends at college.

Today, like all our days, has been a really busy one. Everyone is preparing for the big day—the inauguration. My days are spent helping out in the scheduling office. At least we have a nice hotel to fall asleep in each night! I'll call you this weekend.

Love,
Faye

It is January 17, 1993, three days before the president's Inauguration Day. We continue to be inundated with endless inquiries about what the inaugural celebration will entail, who will be where, details about the various inaugural balls, and which balls will the president and first lady attend?

This week has been a whirlwind. One month from now, or even a week from now, I won't remember most of the tasks I've been charged with performing. Every media inquiry sounds like the last one or the one before. There are few new or interesting questions.

The excitement of this new experience, this new environment, the amazing people I've met should allow me the pleasure of overlooking or masking my fear. But it doesn't. I'm very much aware that this beautiful, vibrant, yet cold city will change my life. I'm just not sure whether it will be for the better.

It will take me weeks before I learn my way around, but I don't have that kind of time to spare. Everything is in accelerated mode and was needed yesterday. I am grateful for the ordinary things that most people in this city take for granted—the amazingly efficient subway and bus system; the taxis that will take you anywhere you want to go any time of the day or night; and the downtown stores that are just blocks from our offices. This is a city built and operated for the benefit of busy and important people.

In the midst of my trepidation, excitement, fears and grief, I am also grateful that my flight to Washington went fine. The hotel is wonderful and spacious, and Bob is here.

January 20—the day we, and the world, have been waiting for. We arrive at the office at 7 a.m., and the phones are already ringing off the hook. The faxes are spewing nonstop inquiries. It is, categorically, a mad house. Every news outlet in the world wants any bit of information it can get about this day. It is far busier than any of the other days leading up to it.

Finally, just before the inauguration begins, the magic hour arrives. Just around 11 a.m., we all depart our temporary office . . . in transit to the real office. We pack our folders and papers before hurrying—as if the "Pumpkin Coach" is about to leave us—for the train station. The train drops us off just blocks from the White House.

Today, we are all too excited to remember how exhausted we are. There are hundreds of thousands of overexcited people in this small space called Washington, D.C. We look at each other, smiling, amazed. We had no idea the crowd would already be out in full force or that it would be this huge.

We are forced to elbow our way toward the northwest gate at 17th and Pennsylvania. We were forewarned that there is no other way for us to get into the White House. Everyone—no matter who—must be cleared by the security guards before entering the White House.

As I make my way to the gate, I am thinking back over the last few days. I am certain that these days were not as disconcerting for my younger colleagues. I feel a small stab of guilt and self-pity. They wouldn't know that I'd spent these few days trying to understand why I am here, whether the final decision to come here was the right one.

And I would never tell anyone how often I prayed about this decision. Now, it is January 20, and I am telling myself that it was the right decision, that God must have a reason to bring this sharecropper's daughter all the way to the White House.

───✦

Except for postcards, textbook pictures and images from the television screen, January 20, 1993, was the first time I'd actually set eyes on the White House in my 39 years. It was my first day on the job as a White House Media Affairs officer. I would never be able to live through another January 20th—even if I lived to be 100 years old— without remembering that day.

The scene at the northwest gate was chaotic, as the White House guards worked as fast as they could to identify the new Clinton staff and to clear us all as close to noon as possible. Noon, January 20th. It's the magical hour in presidential politics; the changing of the guard in Washington, D.C.—out with the old, in with the new, except for the times when presidents remain in office for a second term.

I wondered if this day was going smoother for the men and women leaving the White House. While we, the new inhabitants, had to go through the process of becoming part of the White House system, they, the former inhabitants, only had to be purged from the system, pack their bags, figuratively speaking, and wave goodbye.

I was relieved to learn that I was already in the system. The guard looked briefly up at me, typed a few words into his computer and deemed me "cleared" for entrance into the White House. There was still a long line of new White House staffers not yet cleared. They stood, frowning, impatient and exhausted as they peered into the gate.

Some of the guards were gruff and short with their answers. Most, though, were nice, even joking about the "first-day blues." After clearing me, the young guard hurried outside the guard shack and showed me "the right way" to swipe the badge across the monitor. The turnstile that would allow me into the White House grounds magically turned.

The blue pass I hung around my neck had a giant "W" across it. This was a temporary pass. It had no name, no picture and no office. It meant we were cleared officially, but temporarily.

We would become permanent official White House employees after going through the lengthy vetting process that precipitated FBI clearance. According to veteran White House aides, the FBI would turn over and investigate every document our names showed up on—financial records, school records, speeding tickets . . . even the ticket I received when my wayward dog dug out of the back gate and freely roamed Vancouver Drive. I'd had to appear in court for that one.

The FBI would send investigators to my Arkansas neighborhood to ask questions—especially of former spouses and next-door neighbors. The investigators sought, to the best of their ability, assurances that the people honored with White House employee status were neither criminals, nor harbingers of secret and embarrassing pasts. There were only a few crevices I hoped they'd overlook.

There were fewer of us waiting to get inside the White House than those who were simply standing and watching as the changing of the guard took place. Though we didn't have giant D's on our foreheads and the guys walking out didn't have R's, we all knew. This quasi-ceremonial change was as much a part of Inauguration Day as the president's inaugural ceremony.

I was finally inside the northwest gate. I stopped, looking back to see the familiar faces still standing outside. I looked ahead of me at the White House, savoring this moment to share with D.K. and Daddy when I wrote or called to tell them about Inauguration Day.

I would recall this moment each time I thought of why it was worth it to take this giant step in my life. I would mentally pull out this snapshot whenever I questioned whether I had done the right thing—leaving my home and my family and friends back in Arkansas. I would tuck it in a safe place to share with grandchildren one day.

As we walked in, the Bush administration staff members were walking out, turning in their White House passes for the last time. It was one of those otherworldly feelings again. As the men and women running the country one day ago walked out and left it to the new guard that was us. Most of them hardly glanced our way, but some of them did, and it seemed their eyes would momentarily settle on me.

There were thousands of people—every age, ethnicity, size and shape—lining the D.C. streets on Inauguration Day. More people than I had ever imagined came for presidential inaugurations, and certainly more people than I'd seen at any political function before. There would be no reports of violence or criminal activities in spite of the crowds. Everyone seemed bent on witnessing and enjoying this historic day.

By all accounts, the audience at the inauguration of America's 42nd president on January 20, 1993, was made up of more blacks and minorities than any presidential inauguration in American history—including Kennedy, Johnson and Roosevelt. The universal pride, hope and, yes, patriotism in the air was palpable. Our own Bill Clinton from a place called Hope brought hope to the White House with him.

I later realized that the younger White House staffers were very interested in how and how well I knew our new president. The strange look on some of their faces told me they didn't realize just how small Arkansas really was—small enough for lots of people to know our former governor.

─────

The inaugural ceremony was in full swing by the time our group arrived inside the White House. We stopped in the lower press office to watch the ceremony on television. We could feel the excitement and electricity in the air, even through the television screen.

Our eyes were glued to the TV attached high upon the wall. The first family—President Clinton, first lady Hillary, and Chelsea—were walking down the capital mall. A long, sleek black limousine followed them, while the handsome, Secret Service agents walked instep just behind the first family.

It had been difficult convincing people who didn't know him that Bill Clinton was presidential material—not just whites, but blacks, as well. They all had preconceived notions about Southerners, in general, and Southern white politicians, in particular. It wasn't a personal indictment of Bill Clinton; it was simply the country's prejudice about Arkansas' capability to breed a leader of the free world.

Inauguration Day was redemption. It was a good feeling to see our Bill Clinton about to take the helm, to lead America into a new century and to work to keep his promises to America. He was being launched into a role that few people—except for Bill Clinton, himself; his mother, Virginia Kelly; and the loyal Arkansans who had witnessed his brilliant leadership—ever believed he could pull off.

As we sat silently watching the ceremony, the applause and cheers were deafening. My few tears were shed in silence and in private. Maya Angelou's inaugural poem "On the Pulse of Morning" beautifully insinuated what I felt, that Bill Clinton's victory was about so much more than a political election and about so many more Americans than the ones who were involved in that election.

How appropriate that Maya, an Arkansan with such a rich past, would recite the inaugural poem. She not only paid homage to an Arkansas politician who became president of the United States; but also to the Stamps, Arkansas, grandmother who helped raise her and forced her to recognize her worth, in spite of a scarred childhood. Maya Angelou was claiming Arkansas, the South, and William Jefferson Clinton as her own. Her deep, life-enhanced voice resonated throughout the mall and the crowds beyond.

⁕

After the inauguration, we walked through the halls of the West Wing, then outside and into the Old Executive Office Building next door. While a few from our group remained in the West Wing press office, the majority of us—Media Affairs officers—would be housed in the Old Executive Office Building.

We had heard the joke about White House real estate and realized the irony. The West Wing consisted of a few small offices along with a handful of mostly cramped cubicles. They were, however, just a skip and a hop from the Oval Office.

The Old Executive Office Building, on the other hand, was a beautiful, stately building with wide, shiny hallways and open, spacious offices. The high windows offered amazing views of the White House grounds and of Washington.

We each dropped our belongings near an empty desk in one of the empty offices and wandered through the halls of the White House like characters in "Alice in Wonderland," searching for some hint of the people who were there before. But there was little left behind.

There was, in fact, nothing real about that day. We weren't even permanent White House employees yet, just curious seekers of what this new place was all about.

In some strange sense, the 10 men and women who would become the White House Media Affairs office bonded in those moments. We became the new keepers of this White House domain. Jeff Eller would be the wizard with the controls.

The strangest part about that historic day was how we were directed to furnish our offices—a genuine White House scavenger hunt. It was the tradition, Jeff laughed, crossing his heart and "hoping to die."

"Either drag what you want back to your office," Jeff said, "or stick your name on it in big, bold letters . . . maybe nobody will bother it."

We rambled up and down the floors seeking out the furniture we wanted in our offices. We were putting that old American tradition of "first come, first serve" into action.

Later that evening, after an afternoon of eerie, humorous activities in the White House, I sat and thought about just how miraculous the day had been—for me personally, and for the country. I was, again, fighting back the tears that threatened to show the others what a big deal this was for me.

By the end of the day of celebrations, it was becoming abundantly clear that I was a long way from Little Rock, Arkansas . . . and even farther from Varner Road. D.C. was a world away from what I'd known all my life, or even just a few days earlier.

I was no longer simply Janis Kearney, the small newspaper publisher from Little Rock, Arkansas. I was now a member of a very elite group of people—White House aides. Even though there was a sizable gap between me and the men and women at the top of that elite group, still, I was a member of that group.

This was a sobering thought, one that might have resulted in a swollen ego, except there was too much behind me. There were too many people I owed this awesome experience to—my father and my mother, for sure. How I wished she was here to share this chapter of my life. The fact that she wasn't left a painful void.

My mother was the one who convinced me that going away to college was not only non-negotiable, but also that I'd grow with the experience, once I allowed myself to do so. Yet, it was very scary taking that long trip up to Fayetteville in the northwest Arkansas hills. To me, the University of Arkansas was more than just four hours away; it was on the other side of the world. That distance had filled my 17-year-old being with fear and uncertainties.

Mama would be more than just proud; she would be excited about this new turn in my life. A Yellow Dog Democrat to her bones, she would have rooted for Bill Clinton from the beginning, talked him up to her friends and encouraged her church sisters and brothers to vote "the right way." And she would have touted the fact that we'd at last have an Arkansan—and a good president—in the White House.

At the same time, she would never let me forget that other passion in her life, faith. She would have reminded me that, in the end, none of our successes or our victories is possible without God. At the end of the most amazing day in my lifetime, I was hoping with all my heart that she knew I hadn't forgotten.

Washington was no Little Rock. I'd have to change a few things about myself to make it in the nation's capital. Bob had told me I'd have to shed some of the Arkansas garb and arm myself with tougher armor.

"I know you don't like politics, Janis, but you chose to be in the middle of it."

While D.C. was much more than I'd bargained for, I would refuse to allow it to be more than I could handle. Daddy had taught us well when he told us, "If you dream it, you better be ready to live through it." And I would.

January 20, 1993

Hi Daddy,

I am so tired I could fall asleep standing up. What a day! I'm not sure I can describe it to you. All day, I was thinking to myself that less than 20 years ago, I was home in Gould picking cotton and chopping cotton, and today . . . I'm watching a presidential inauguration in real life! I really wish you and Mama could have been right here with me, today.

There were more people in this town than I think I've ever seen in my whole life. I can tell you there were more black folks at this presidential inauguration than at any one before — counting Kennedy, Johnson and Roosevelt. Everybody walked around with a big smile on their face as if today was too good to be true. Bill Clinton is like a dream president for many people all over this country. None of us can believe he actually won.

All day I was surrounded by a crowd of young, enthusiastic white kids. Most of them were younger than 25 years old. But it felt as if we were all in this together. I don't think any of us really thought much about our differences. We were all watching Bill Clinton and feeling good about all the right things he was promising for this country. I was especially proud that he is someone I know.

You should have heard the applause and cheers. And, yes, I couldn't help but cry as I thought about where I came from, how unreal it is for me to be sitting here. Maya Angelou gave a long, beautiful poem. Did you know she lived with her grandmother in Stamps, Arkansas?

Daddy, there's a lot I have to tell you about this day; but I think I'll call it a night and get some sleep. The morning will be here before I know it, and we have so much to do to get our offices in shape for real work. Say hi to everybody. I'll write again real soon.

Love,
Faye

I awoke to another gray morning, in our small bedroom inside the small home in northeast D.C. I still had to remember where I was each morning. I hoped this would change eventually. Being an early riser had never left me and turned out to be a huge positive in my new world of working at the White House. It was February already. Where had the days gone?

It was by sheer luck that I met an NBC cameraman while working at the Clinton-Gore Campaign. He and his sister happened to own a small home in northeast D.C. While ours had been a casual conversation, it turned out to be a very providential one.

The house was just a couple of blocks from the Metro that would take us all the way downtown. Bob and I were pleasantly surprised at the small bungalow on Chillum Place. It was cozy, homey and reminiscent of the type of homes seen on the "Ozzie and Harriet" television series.

Even though the furnishings were vintage '50s and '60s, I was more than grateful that I wouldn't have to spend hours shopping for new furniture. The house was perfect for two people whose waking hours were almost all devoted to their jobs.

Once we left home, Bob and I would see little of each other during our long days, even though we worked just one floor apart. We'd quickly learned to separate our personal lives from the very public ones at the White House.

We left home each morning at 6:15 a.m. for the 10-minute walk to the Totten Road train station. We'd follow a narrow dirt path—a short cut that trailed behind tall, old buildings that must have once housed factories or offices.

Later, after I'd brought my Mitsubishi to D.C., we sometimes drove the few blocks if we were running late. On those days, we left the car in the Park-and-Kiss parking lot across from the station.

Our train was rarely more than a couple of minutes late, arriving at our stop most mornings around 6:30 a.m. Thirty minutes later, we were deposited at the downtown Farragut Street station. It was always a struggle for us to get out the door before the automated voice told us "The doors are closing." At that time of the morning, everyone seemed to be dashing for the Farragut stop.

It took us another 10-minute walk directly up 17th Street to get to the White House from the station. During our brief walk, we'd mumble a few sentences as we passed drug stores, office buildings, small restaurants, and homeless people still asleep on benches or lying on the ground wrapped in cover or clothing.

It was as if there was an unspoken pact that we not mention how eerily different our new lives were from the ones we both knew back in Arkansas. At 7:15 a.m., we would finally arrive at the gates of the White House.

On that particular February morning, I'd slowly awakened from a strange, but familiar dream that caused both angst and some peculiar sense of comfort. I was disoriented as I shook away the cobwebs, realizing that in this dream, I was Faye, the child, not Janis, the grown-up. I was at home on Varner Road—safe, secure, happy.

I lay in bed beside Bob, who was still sleeping, as I tried to recall the dream. Before I rushed off to take a quick shower and dress for work, I lay there for another moment—the extent of our time for lazing most mornings.

Slowly, the dream unraveled before my mind's eye. My subconscious had kindly settled me in the place and time that afforded me the most comfort and security. In the dream, both of my parents were smiling and talking animatedly, though I didn't know the subject of their conversation. It was that early period of my life before I began to experience some of the pains or even the joys of life outside that cocoon.

I was not completely clueless as to why the dream took place. I was grateful. A part of me wanted to revert back to that simpler existence, to bypass the many changes that were taking place in my life.

My first months in Washington were overwhelming; and, as much as I hated to admit it, I was on the edge of depression. It was far more of a culture shock than I'd prepared myself for. Maybe a better word would be separation shock—from all I loved and all I knew. Where was the sense of excitement I usually felt in delving into something new?

Certainly, part of my mood swing was from an overload of changes. The cold, gray weather that came with this new month stayed with us for several weeks. Much of my lack of spirit was just from missing home, my family and friends. As my siblings often accused me of doing as a child, I might have been "making a mountain out of a molehill."

The dream reminded me, again, how far from my old world I had traveled and that this new home was something I'd have to learn from scratch. Here, finally, I'd met a change that was neither easy, nor fun. If I allowed it to be so, I knew it could be exciting; but I wasn't there, yet.

More than a few times, I seriously considered returning home. The only thing that prevented me from doing it was the thought of being a quitter—giving up before I gave D.C. and myself a real chance to grow on each other. I was very disappointed that I hadn't made the necessary transformation sooner, just days after setting foot in the city.

The last thing I wanted to do was worry Bob with what I had determined was my childish fears and concerns. Eventually, though, I did. He didn't understand. It was more like he couldn't believe I was serious. Nevertheless, he assured me the feeling would pass, that I was just being overly sensitive.

"Give it some time . . . all of this will pass," he said encouragingly.

I promised him I would do just that, not at all sure it would make a difference. Unlike me, Bob wasn't a novice to either politics or Washington. He had lived in Washington while attending Howard University's graduate school in the '70s. He loved politics with a passion, more than I ever would. It wasn't just that he understood politics better, which he did; but he also gained enjoyment in the day-to-day process.

Although he would never whine about it, I imagined he, surely, was having some adjustment moments, too. We had both left our families, homes, and friends behind. We both had lives that we'd enjoyed and would never have abandoned had Bill Clinton not won the presidency.

I was grateful for this amazing opportunity just as Bob was. But clearly I was not ready to take full advantage of the opportunity, as he was. Bob encouraged me, though, to learn the game and try my very best to enjoy it. He warned me that either I get used to politics and find a way to enjoy it, or I would always be unhappy here.

I'm trying. I'm trying very hard, I'd tell him. But it always seemed that there was too much to learn, too much to get used to. No one had told me people would be so ... different from those I'd left in Arkansas. I wasn't forewarned that friendships here were not the same as friendships where I came from, or that success in the nation's capital was as much a result of how well one honed their skills at politics as how well they learned their jobs.

My mantra each day was "I am extremely lucky, extremely blessed. This is an honor!" It wasn't just a mantra. It was true. Bob and I were a part of a miniscule group of African Americans—no, of Americans, who could say they worked in the White House and knew the president personally. What in the world was there not to feel lucky about?

When I complained, my new friends—most of who were veteran politicians—laughed as if I were missing a marble or two. The look on their faces expressed an adult's pity for a child who doesn't know the simple rules of riding a bike and staying upright.

"You *really do* get used to it," they'd say. I saw this as their form of a pat on the head. I'm sure that is a good thing, the getting used to it and becoming a pro at the political game.

It's definitely a whole new world.

"It's Washington, not Arkansas," I kept hearing.

During my first three months in Washington, I remained at the Media Affairs office. My title was deputy director of the Specialty Press office. I worked in a huge room in the Old Executive Office Building, which housed the majority of the White House staff.

My office mates included the office supervisor, Maria Tio, an African American woman born in New Orleans; and Josh Silverman, a young Jewish man who I worked closely with in our day-to-day media coordination roles.

Our jobs during the early months were nonstop. We arrived at the office before 7 a.m. each day for a morning meeting and began work after 30 minutes of updates on the president's schedule, his short-term and long-term calendar, and the specific media projects demanding our immediate attention.

My job included setting up interviews with specialty media—any media that were not mainstream daily newspapers or the larger television networks or publications. We coordinated media queries, wrote and distributed media kits and set up interviews with White House staff. Our projects took every minute of our day and often well into the night. It was a given that we would work on Saturdays and part of many Sundays.

Jeff Eller, who was considered a brilliant media and communications manager, was a workaholic. This, of course, was not different from the rest of the men and women who ran the White House offices. It was a prerequisite, especially in the early days. We were all learning ... making mistakes and learning the right way to do things the next time.

Maria Tio, a former broadcast journalist, and Jeff Eller knew each other from their broadcast days in Florida. They were both a long way from home, too. Most of us were. Of the 10 people who made up the Media Affairs office, most were younger than Jeff, Maria and me. They were all hard-working, smart and committed to the Clinton presidency. From what I had heard, that same young group partied as hard as they worked. As an almost-married woman in her late 30s, I wasn't privy to those outings.

I was especially fond of two young men who I got to know back in Arkansas during the campaign. Richard Strauss was 22 years old and his new position was head of the White House Radio office. His good friend, David Anderson, was a year younger and ran the White House Television office. They were both extremely bright and extremely loyal to President Clinton and his administration.

New jobs always caused me temporary stress, so why would I have expected anything different in a new job at the White House during those first few months of 1993? Especially, given the fact that practically every single one of us was new at working in the White House, and we were all learning by doing—sometimes getting it right, sometimes not.

Add to that "newbies" curve, the fact that we had to quickly learn the subtleties of White House office politics, how to deal with people in other parts of the

White House, and how to deal with people outside the White House who oftentimes were only interested in you because you work in the White House.

There are, undoubtedly, many books written to guide new White House employees through the travails of early days at the White House. But I didn't have access to them during the first months of 1993.

While bringing our work home was surely detrimental to our relationship, few White House employees have the privilege of leaving their work at the office—certainly not presidential appointees. We all signed on for what we knew could result in eight-hour days, or just as easily, 12-hour days.

Bob and I saw each other in the mornings, rode together to the White House, and sometimes rode together back to our home. Very seldom did we spend time together during the day, and very often, by the time we were both home, it seemed it was time to sleep then get up again.

It was also in the middle of learning my way in that Wonderland that I remembered my promise to Daddy; that I would try my very best to visit at least every other month. Why would I have made such an impossible promise in the first place?

Thankfully, Daddy never held me to my promise, although, knowing him, he never forgot it, either. The guilt of leaving would set in during those times. I had brothers who were great at being there for Daddy, but he had depended on a female throughout his 45 years of marriage, then the 10 years with me trying to walk in Mama's shoes. Daddy believed that being a caretaker was definitely a female responsibility.

It wasn't easy to tell my father that Bob and I were living together. It didn't matter that I was almost 40 years old and had been married before, for 16 years. While I was not like my mom in the traditional sense, I knew that Daddy was. And I wrestled with telling him I was—from his viewpoint—"living in sin."

The truth was that Bob's and my decision to live together was, to a great extent, based on economics. The cost of living was almost twice what it was in Arkansas. We were saving in a lot of ways. Arkansans who uprooted families or just themselves to come to D.C. went through a major price shock. I'd tell Daddy that we were talking about marriage, and it would likely happen soon.

I took Bob's and other former White House aides' advice to try and enjoy my experience inside the White House, but to make an exit strategy as soon as I could.

"It won't take you long to find out it's not all the glamour people think it is," they said. "You'll want to find a good job out in one of the departments . . . they pay better, and it's a lot less stress."

I continued working in the Media Affairs office until March of that year, just as I was learning my job and beginning to gain some enjoyment in it. I often bumped into the president during my days as he hosted foreign leaders in the Oval Office or made speeches in the Rose Garden. He was always happy to see Arkansans, to chat just for a moment about home. He was amazingly generous in recognizing us, introducing us to White House visitors, whether they were from another part of the country or another side of the world.

One day, as I stood in the back of the Oval Office during an official meeting, he beckoned me to come over.

"This is Janis Kearney. She came from Arkansas with me. I know the whole family . . . her parents were sharecroppers. Theirs is an amazing story, all 17 children graduated from college."

In spite of all the new information he now had to stuff inside his brains and the burden of running the free world, Bill Clinton held onto the small details of the world he'd known before becoming president.

He remained an amazing walking encyclopedia filled with big and little details. He never forgot that each of my siblings' names began with J or the conversation he had with my father after his second term as governor, or how four Kearney brothers—and now one sister—had worked for him during his political career.

One of my brothers headed up a state agency and served as a public service commissioner. Another was appointed governor's liaison for two agencies, then appointed as a juvenile judge.

Yet another brother headed up the state's ethics commission. I was the lone Kearney female to work for Bill Clinton and serve in the White House. A younger brother, however, worked in his presidential transition office and later was appointed deputy secretary for international trade at the Department of Commerce.

During my months inside the Clinton White House, I never became disillusioned about why Bill Clinton was there. And we certainly didn't have time to get bored. Once I began to accept change, I recognized just how exciting working at the White House was. There was something new and exciting happening every day . . . every hour.

I spent many mornings in the office of the Old Executive Office Building, which was referred to as simply OEOB, where the health care briefings were held, listening to the impassioned conversations about what was needed to assure universal health care. I was so confident that health care would be a wonderful part of the Clinton legacy when they left the White House. I knew there were few things more important to the American people.

It was especially inspiring to observe Mrs. Clinton as she sometimes walked with her aides and assistants from the residence to the meeting room. Sometimes she simply sat quietly, whispering to whoever sat beside her. Other times, she participated or led the discussions.

Those were memorable times. Mrs. Clinton's passion and compassion about health care reform was invigorating, reaffirming. My heart swelled with pride as she spoke so eloquently about something that hit home with me and the communities I knew best. Affordable health care was such a realistic goal. I wondered how any lawmaker could argue the validity of this issue?

Even with Bob's and others' advice to leave the White House sooner than later, the one deciding factor in my leaving sooner than I might have was a need for more pay. The White House salary was less than adequate for most adults who were not already wealthy or still living off wealthy parents, or those who could afford to make a lot less for a while. I was none of the above. I still had bills that the income from my struggling newspaper wouldn't begin to cover.

As excited and committed as I was about my role in the White House, it took me only weeks to realize why the employees were disproportionately young, college graduates who were new to the job market or the children of wealthy families. These were the groups who could best afford to work in the White House and live off the restrictive salaries.

The rest of us, unless we held the top positions, simply couldn't afford to serve at this coveted address for very long. On top of the already restrictive salaries, our president went a step farther and cut salaries by 25 percent and froze increases—leaving very little leeway for empathetic bosses who wanted to help. Gratefully, I was given a small raise early on, but even that didn't meet all my needs.

In early March, a good friend, Alvin Brown, who worked in the personnel office, dropped by my office and asked if I would consider a communications role in one of the agencies. He'd heard "through the grapevine" that I might be open to such a move.

"Would you be interested in interviewing for such a position . . . maybe director of communications?"

I beamed. "That would be great! Where is it?"

"It's at the Small Business Administration. I thought it might be a good match since communications is your background, and you're a genuine small business owner." He wrote the name of the contact person and her phone number on a slip of paper, before handing it to me.

"Katie Broren. She's cool. She'll be calling you today or tomorrow."

"Thanks. I'll look forward to hearing from her."

The next day the phone rang, and a chirpy female voice on the other end introduced herself as "Katie . . . Alvin's friend over here at SBA."

After a short chat, we agreed I'd come the next day for an interview. That next day, I worked through my lunch break, and by early afternoon I reminded Maria, the office supervisor, that I was taking a late lunch.

I caught one of the hundreds of taxis that lined up outside the OEOB and asked the driver to take me to "403 C Street, Southwest, please." I was reading from the scrap of paper Alvin had left me. The 15-minute taxi ride ended at an auspicious building that took up a full block.

"This is Design Center, Miss." I was sure the taxi driver was responding to my curious stare. "You look for office, here?"

"Yes, the Small Business Administration."

He nodded. "Yes, SBA inside. Someone tell you which floor."

I thanked the taxi driver, left a small tip and hurried into the building. I saw the agency's information desk as soon as I walked through the revolving doors. "May I help you?" asked a woman who stood at the counter with a friendly smile. I told her my name and said that I was there to see Katie Broren. She smiled, wrote "9th Floor Visitor" on a name tag and handed it to me.

"You should keep this on while you're here. Please sign the visitors' roster, and I'll call Katie to let her know you're on your way up." I smiled and nodded as she pointed me toward the elevator.

Katie was friendly, inquisitive and more than willing to answer my questions about the history of the Small Business Administration. She told me she had worked with the Clinton-Gore Campaign, "not in the headquarters, of course," she quickly added, but in Denver and mostly doing advance work.

I wasn't surprised. Although she had an infectious kind of chirpiness, she also exhibited an advance person's take-charge, blunt way of interacting with strangers. Many of my political associates and friends were advance types, and they'd made me understand that the take-charge bluntness came with having to deal with all kinds of people "from nice types to creeps."

Katie and I talked more than I would have expected about the campaign, some about the history of the SBA and some about the White House's relationship with the agency. Before we knew it, the interview was over.

"You've done this kind of work before, right . . . I'm going by your resume."

Surprised at this new kind of interview, I nodded. "Yes, I've done everything's that's on my resume and more," I laughed.

"Alrighty then. Thanks, Janis. I have a few other interviews this week, but I'll be calling everyone early next week."

Spring was just around the corner, but just before its official debut, we would experience a true Washington winter. Lucky us, we had arrived in D.C. during one of the area's roughest winters in years.

Snowstorms raged, and most schools in surrounding counties were closed as much as five days. The snowdrifts neared 20 inches in some places. The government closed down, causing a barrage of op-eds and front-page complaints about the city government's continued failures. Even during the government closing, Bob and I and some others trudged into work by bus or train.

On March 15, 1993, Katie called. "You ready to come over and take over the SBA's communications office?" she asked in her still chirpy voice. I smiled so wide I was sure she probably could see it.

"Gosh, yes . . . when should I plan on coming aboard?"

"We'll have to finish getting all your paperwork in place this week. You should plan to start first thing next week, but why don't you come over tomorrow or the next day to meet with the acting administrator. You can meet your staff, too." That call started in motion my shuffle between the White House and the SBA.

"You sure you're ready to leave the White House now?" Bob asked the day I told him about Katie's call.

"I'm sure . . . it's time," I'd responded.

He didn't bother to say "I told you so," even though he'd left weeks earlier for his new appointment as undersecretary at the U.S. Department of Agriculture.

Bob and I drove to my new workplace the weekend before I went to work there; then we caught the train to see just how long it would take. The agency was a 30-minute train ride from our home on Chillum Place. By my last week at the White House, I was so excited about the move, I had cleaned out my desk days early.

Jeff Eller was very supportive and understanding about my move, although he joked a few times that I was jumping ship. I'd been upfront about my salary needs and that I would be looking for a job outside the White House. Jeff had given me a stellar recommendation when Katie had called to inquire about me, she later told me.

"Thanks for all your good work, Janis."

Jeff wasn't one to give out compliments, which made me that much more appreciative of him. I was sent off with a small, informal gathering of Media Affairs staffers and volunteers and a few other White House friends who dropped by to wish me well. I was really going to miss Dave Anderson and Richard Strauss. Not long out of college, the two were exceedingly intelligent and creative, but also demonstrated a wild sense of humor that kept me in stitches.

I was just one in the first wave of veteran Clinton White House expatriates to leave the coveted address for a less ostentatious address. Historically, few people remain where they start out in presidential administrations, and even fewer stay with an administration beyond 18 months. The Clinton White House set a record for cabinet members and senior administrators remaining in their jobs longer than White House aides before them.

I left the White House on March 19 to become communications manager with the U.S. Small Business Administration. That day was such an exciting one, I couldn't understand why there was this little dark cloud that seemed to be following me around all day. It was near noon before I realized that it was the 11th anniversary of my mother's passing. Some place deep in my subconscious would always acknowledge that momentous date.

While I would miss the excitement of working inside the White House, the most important address in the country, I was slowly learning that you gave up some things for such exclusive privileges. I was looking forward to my new job heading up SBA's communications office and having some semblance of a normal day again.

My doubled salary was undeniably a huge incentive for the optimism I had about this new job. Now, I wouldn't stress about my son's last years in college.

My new presidential appointment was as assistant administrator for public communications for the U.S. Small Business Administration. It was a mouthful that most times I whittled down to "communications director." In fact, the first six months I worked there, I was "acting" assistant administrator as we waited for our permanent administrator, Erskine Bowles, to come aboard. I also had to go through my additional vetting process.

Spring arrived in Washington just a week after one of the worst snowstorms the area had experienced in years. Maybe it was a normal D.C. spring, I thought. Or maybe I was starved for something that reminded me of the springs I'd known in Arkansas—the captivating colors and the warmth of nature.

I know it didn't really happen this way, but it seemed as if I awoke one March morning, looked out my window and was surprised by a perfect, spring day with vibrant bouquets of flowers shifting in the gentle March wind. Even in the places where spots of snow remained on the softening ground, splashes of color peeped out. Birds sang louder songs of welcome, of rebirth.

It was cherry blossom season, the true indication of spring. Even if spring showed its face, then hid again for a while, we knew the season of life was imminent. There are few sights in D.C. that are more awe-inspiring than the cherry blossoms. Travelers from around the country and the world come to pay homage to a city quilted in the beautiful and aromatic pink blossoms. Such a pity this season lasts only a few days; and these amazing decorations disappear so quickly.

Whether it is deserving of my gratitude or not, I will always credit the cherry blossom season for completely transforming me during that first springtime in the District. It was then that I fell madly, irrevocably in love with Washington, D.C, my new home, finally.

When I look back at my first days in the city, there was so much that should have changed my mind right away. I couldn't see it because I was remembering that I was 1,700 miles from Arkansas . . . 1,790 miles from Varner Road.

My stubbornness, though, melted away along with the last winter sludge and the softening of the harsh eastern winds as spring arrived. Our new friends—all migrants from some other part of the country, who had come and stayed—forewarned us about Potomac Fever, saying, "You'll love this place before it's over, and you won't want to leave." Finally, I had an idea of what they meant.

It was like the boy you never imagine falling in love with, even when others tell you how perfect the two of you are for each other. It happens suddenly. One day he is sitting there minding his own business and you notice how his smile lights up his eyes or as he turns his head a certain way, you see a different face from this new angle. And you've gone and done it . . . fallen in love, in spite of yourself.

Suddenly, I was anxious, excited about waking each morning. Now that neither Bob nor I was at the White House, we could actually grab a cup of coffee before leaving for the Metro each morning. We could even browse through the newspaper during our ride downtown. I found myself, strangely, smiling at passengers . . . just feeling alive.

The city awakened, rousing me from my months-long sleep. Even the sounds of the city became suddenly harmonious melodies. As the trees sprouted color and texture, and I began to notice the sweet, intoxicating fragrances of spring, I was, at last, enjoying my new home.

It was in Washington, that I decided that kindness might very well be a seasonal emotion. The once cold, closed faces with uncaring eyes were suddenly open, curious, and bright. The office clerks where we renewed our licenses, or bought our tags, would smile as if they recognized me from another time. There was an energy of good feelings, of happiness in being alive.

Why wouldn't I have noticed how this political axis of power is also an archive of history and culture? Or that there is enough art and music to last several lifetimes or that the Hollywood-like side of D.C. was also alive and well?

The long lines of sleek, shiny limousines were dizzying as they whisked nonstop down Pennsylvania Avenue and K Street. The limousine expo would begin on Thursday and end on Sunday—ushering the rich, powerful and connected to endless black-tie affairs, concerts, theaters, state dinners, power weddings, international summits, conferences, balls, cocktail receptions and inaugurations.

We learned quickly that to arrive in D.C. without a black dress or tuxedo was like vacationing in the Caribbean without a swimsuit. But knowing the right place to be was still the most important prerequisite to acquiring power in Washington.

There is no gray area when it comes to D.C. One can only love or hate the nation's capital. When springtime arrived in D.C., I found myself changing along with the season. I had fought against it; said I never would. But I believed this change was good. The slight bending and blending would allow me to love my new home, my new life, this new world . . . until the next spring.

The first opportunity Bob and I got to visit home was April, just weeks after I began my new job at the SBA. I wanted to return for the anniversary celebration of the Arkansas State Press. My first stop was 2217 Vancouver Drive—home. No one was there. Janetta was now spending most of her time at the newspaper. The quiet inside my home was different from the quiet I once coveted when I lived in it. Then, there were the echoes of voices, laughter, conversations in the hallways, bedrooms, even inside the walls.

There had been an invisible human presence and warmth, in spite of the quiet. On my return, there was just silence. I walked downstairs into the garage and turned the wall light on. The beige Mitsubishi I'd bought in Pine Bluff two years earlier was like the loyal pet awaiting my return.

I'd bought the car after a scary accident in my small Geo Prism. The toy car, as friends described it, was totaled. I'd driven a rental car for weeks until the insurance agent called and said the insurance company wouldn't continue to pay for it. I drove to Pine Bluff with a friend who knew a lot more about automobile purchases than I did. We spent a full afternoon on the grounds test-driving one small car after another.

Finally, the exasperated dealer showed me the champagne-colored Mitsubishi that had been bought and returned with less than 40 miles on the odometer. It was love at first sight, and I followed my friend back to Little Rock in my beautiful new Galant.

Back upstairs, I grabbed the car keys. Now was as good a time as ever to give the car a dose of fresh air. What a strange feeling . . . that I had lost my sense of home in the place I had loved and lived in for so many years. So much of who I am had been formulated within these walls. Had there been so much change in my life in just these last three months? I wondered if D.K. felt as I did. There was some grief in this realization, some sorrow to have lost a part of me that once meant so much.

I walked into the bedroom that once was my sanctuary. In that moment, I realized I might now be without a sanctuary . . . for certain it was no longer at this address.

Back downstairs, I switched on the light. The sight of my car brought the first smile to my face since I'd stepped inside the house. At last, here was something that was still mine, something that hadn't changed in a mere three months.

I drove through Boyle Park, then onto Asher Street. A stranger could drive this route and easily figure out this area's demographics. The community was made up of a mixed bag—poor, working poor, and lower-middle class families. The businesses were just as diverse. Some were high-end discount clothing stores; family restaurants with endless salad bars; fried chicken drive-throughs; and at least one barbecue joint.

There were the warehouse food stores where families bought in bulk, then bagged their own groceries. There were also a handful of ethnic restaurants where a person could make a day's meal out of fried rice, noodles and Mexican food. There was the giant theater for families and the college students who stuck around during the weekends. .

University Avenue was long known for its miles-long stretch of car dealerships where buyers had endless options of choosing the car they wanted and could afford.

The streets were still sparse during the middle of the day. But that would all change in a few hours when a symphony of horns and brakes and voices would bring the area to life as school children, teens and downtown workers made their way home. For the 16 years I'd lived in southwest Little Rock, the streets had been in constant need of repair. Some things hadn't changed in three months.

I drove down Asher Street until it changed to Wright Avenue, five miles of old neighborhoods, corner groceries, a lucrative vegetable market and other small businesses. Across High Street, I continued on to Broadway, which was the second most-traveled street in Quapaw Quarters' historical district. As always, I marvel at the beautiful homes—large Victorians, colonials and bungalows. Even with the transformation of downtown Little Rock in the '60s and '70s, this once all-white community was still a source of pride for the city.

I was on my way home, the only home that would never change for me—Varner Road. I settled myself into the Mitsubishi for the drive down Highway 65. Less than 10 miles south of Pine Bluff, I passed the beautiful Noble Lake. I slowed, enjoying its beauty, but also remembering how the 10- or 12-year-old Janis had looked at this water and seen an ocean. I slowed again, as I passed the small town of Grady, known around the country for its eagle-eyed city policemen. Fifteen minutes later, I was finally slowing for Varner Road.

The drive re-confirmed what I'd always known . . . that the mostly flat, mostly rural state of Arkansas was a natural treasure. It was beautiful in April with its towering trees and flowers announcing a Southern spring. Though I could drive the route with my eyes closed, why would I want to? The route held far too many memories, wonderful memories. No matter how exciting Washington was, I knew I'd left something very special behind.

There was a feeling of comfort in the drive, but also my anticipation of seeing Daddy and Varner Road.

The drives had always served as a vacation from the realities of everyday life, a way to keep me grounded, to hold onto that time that was so important to my life. As long as I didn't let go of what my life had been on Varner Road, I could forge any mountains back in Little Rock, or even in Washington.

The silent drive gave me time to mull over my new life, to try to tally up all that I'd given up, all that I'd gained in the three months since I left home. There was still the nagging question of balance, of wanting to be assured that I didn't lose too much in this journey I'd said "yes" to.

This life of mine, I thought, included long stretches of straight paths, but also the sharp, unexpected turns . . . the newspaper, the campaign, the decision to leave Arkansas . . . and the White House experience. They were all linked to Varner Road, where the journey had, in fact, begun.

I had called earlier to tell Daddy I was on my way, and as always he timed me to make sure I was there by the time he projected. He was standing in the yard as I drove up. We both smiled. He was fine . . . more than fine, this almost 90-year-old father of mine.

Our smiles turned to laughter as I slammed the door shut and hurried toward Daddy. We hugged, and I cried a little. It seemed like years, not months. How I wish I could erase the three months—a lifetime—that had gone between us.

"You made it." Daddy smiled, walking slowly back into his home with me.

"I made it, Daddy. I'm sorry it took me this long. I wish I could have come before now."

Daddy looked away as he walked to the refrigerator for something to snack on.

"Daddy, don't eat too much. Remember, we're going to the newspaper's anniversary reception this evening."

He nodded. "OK, I won't. I know it's hard for you to get away, Faye. I've made myself comfortable with that. I'm just glad to see you whenever you can come down."

The stone in the pit of my stomach was, I knew, the guilt I'd brought with me. I hadn't kept my promise to visit more often. In minutes, Daddy's eyes told me all was forgiven. The stone began to melt. The two hours we spent were so much like the old visits. I had to remind myself that so much had changed, or that Bob and I had to return to D.C.

"It looks like we moving toward getting a new preacher."

"Already? What happened to the old one?"

" We just can't seem to find a preacher that works out. They all start out fine, but soon as they get comfortable, we start to see something we hadn't seen before."

I shook my head smiling, wondering what it would be like if citizens could get rid of their leaders at the drop of a hat the way Daddy and the church got rid of their preachers.

"Maybe you all should just hold off getting the next one, come up with some hard-and-fast requirements this time."

We left for the *State Press*'s annual reception. As Daddy locked his door, I remembered how times had changed. For most of my life, our doors had never been locked. Anytime we visited from college and my parents weren't home, we simply walked right in. Reality had changed that tradition.

"I told folks at church you were here. They were hoping you could come to service."

"Wow . . . I really wish I could, Daddy. But Bob and I have to get back to D.C. tomorrow evening."

"Well, anyway . . . I'm glad you got to come. Everybody's real proud of you, Faye . . . real proud."

We spent the next hour of our drive talking about our new president, about Washington, about how I was finally becoming comfortable with my new home.

Finally, we were back in Little Rock and on our way to the *State Press*.

The *State Press* building was located in the Quapaw Quarters on Broadway Street. It was a small mint-green bungalow set amid larger, more beautiful homes and "quiet" businesses. It was more than adequate for our purposes, and we'd been fortunate to find a home we liked and could afford in this part of the city.

I drove up to the house and smiled to see that my old parking space was no longer mine. As we walked into the office, I saw that things were much the same as I'd left them four months ago. Even the lively flurry of conversations across rooms was reminiscent of my days there. Janetta and Patrice met us at the door, smiling and oohing and aahing over Daddy.

They gave me a hug, still smiling over my shoulder at Daddy. "You look great, Janis . . . D.C. agrees with you!" I smiled graciously, knowing they wouldn't have thought so just a month ago. Daddy, they declared, looked 30 years younger than his age. Daddy smiled; he was use to the compliments, but enjoying them just the same. Finally, he was escorted to a comfortable chair in the front office.

"Why didn't you call to tell us you were on your way, girl?" Janetta asked, smiling.

It was too late for an answer, I decided. "How are you guys holding up?" I walked over to hug Josephine, Danny, and Arnold.

"We're doing fine ... just great," Patrice responded. Everyone else smiled and nodded.

I walked into my old corner office, reminding myself that it was no longer mine. Patrice stood in the doorway, smiling awkwardly.

"I tried not to change too much. I wanted to make sure everything was in its proper place when you return." We both laughed nervously.

"We were all really hoping you had decided you wanted to stay when you came down. And, I admit, I've been doing a little praying ..." Patrice, a devoutly religious woman, half joked.

Guests were starting to arrive, including Bob, who had spent the morning with his own family. The reception celebrating another year of the *Arkansas State Press* was under way. Patrice and Janetta walked together to the front to welcome the guests.

Bob found me still standing in the corner office. He smiled and put his arm around me as I stood at the window, looking out upon the brisk traffic on Broadway Street.

"How does it feel?" he asked.

I wasn't sure. I was home, inside this corner office that had been another sanctuary in my life, a comforting cocoon for a time. The question had made me realize what was missing—that sense of home, of familiarity. How could this happen in so short a time? My home and my newspaper no longer spelled home.

"It's good to be home. I miss the newspaper and everyone here," I answered. In my heart, I wondered if I'd ever return to the newspaper, as I'd told myself I would after the election. Had I traveled too far, now? Oh, how passionately I'd loved this place, this newspaper. The ink had coursed wildly through my veins for five years.

Now, it seemed as if that chapter in my life, those years had been a link to something else. It was hard to fathom. Being publisher of the *Arkansas State Press* had fulfilled me like nothing else had. Yet, the adventurer in me knew my journey would never lead me backward.

I spent much of that afternoon talking with Mrs. Bates and Daddy in between their visiting with each other. Mrs. Bates was one of Daddy's civil rights heroes, and he welcomed the opportunity to talk with her.

When I sat down beside her and gave her another hug, she peered into my eyes and asked if I was happy. I had visited my friend and mentor before leaving for D.C., trying my best to explain my decision to leave the newspaper and follow what I thought I was supposed to be doing at this time in my life.

I had been relieved to see the smile and the understanding in her eyes. She was excited and happy for me. That, however, didn't still the small voice inside my head: Would she see my departure as an abandonment of the newspaper?

Now, she was smiling over at me and patting my knee. "Are you happy, Janis?"

"Almost . . . it's taken me a while to feel comfortable away from home. Finally, I am. But, I'm not sure happy is the right word, yet, Mrs. Bates. I'm glad I'm there, and I do believe I'm supposed to be there."

She nodded, that way she had as she listened and accepted my answer. After a moment of silence she spoke, sharing something about her past I'd never realized.

"You know, I was about your age when I left Arkansas and went to Washington. I spent a year there, during the Johnson administration. I remember how setting foot there was like stepping into another world; different from everything I'd known. You find out, after a while, that it's not as different as we first believe . . . it just takes time."

I smiled and bent to kiss her soft, rouged, cheek.

"Thank you for everything, Mrs. Bates. I will never stop being grateful for what you have done for me," I whispered before leaving her to her throng of fans.

The beautiful civil rights icon looked into my face, patted my face and winked as I left to make room for the rapidly growing crowd of admirers Daisy Bates always attracted. When I looked over at her later, she was in a lively discussion with one of the *State Press* awards recipients, smiling for the camera and looking stunning in her bright red suit.

April 25, 1993

Dear Daddy,

We're back in Washington. We arrived back on time Sunday night. It was so good to see you! I was so happy to see you've been taking care of yourself—or Miss Mary's been taking care of you (smile). Please let her know how much ease she's giving me so far away from home.

I was telling you how I'm beginning to like Washington a lot better as time goes on. As Bob and I touched down on Sunday night, it was my first time really noticing how beautiful this city is. I don't think I've told you much about our place here. It's a little bungalow in northeast D.C. I think it was one of the early black communities where government workers moved. Our neighbors are mostly retirees, and they spend a lot of time working in their yards, or sitting on their porches when the weather's nice.

There're not many children on our street, but there is a high school not far away. We walk through the neighborhoods a lot, but it's not like the South where people spend most of the day outside. Even children aren't outside playing like they do back home.

Daddy, I apologize for waiting to tell you Bob and I are living together. Not that we're some teeny-boppers, but I should have mentioned it to you sooner. It doesn't mean we're definitely headed for marriage, but it just makes sense since we're both here and the cost of living is so high.

I wish D.K. had been home, but he'll be here for the whole summer. It was especially good talking politics with you this time, because I could speak with a little authority for a change, and we also could actually say something positive about the president, for a change (smile).

Bob is enjoying his new job at the Agriculture Department. We're settling in fine and looking forward to the time you can come up and visit. Have to get to bed and set the clock for an early morning.

Love,
Faye

By the summer of 1994, Bob and I were settled into our home on Chillum Road. So settled, in fact, that when we were asked about hosting the Kearney reunion in July of that year, we only hesitated for a moment. We agreed that it was a good time for my family to visit, and they would love all of Washington's history, culture and art.

While we hadn't yet toured any of the historical sites, the reunion would give us a good excuse to do just that. My brother Jude and his wife, Lorraine, lived close by in Silver Springs, Maryland. They readily agreed to co-sponsor the reunion with us.

"We'll do it," we'd told the Arkansas family members who had, for years now, been unfairly saddled with sponsoring the reunions. We would never have been able to take on something so labor intensive and time-consuming if Jude and Lorraine weren't in the area, or if both of us were still at the White House.

Though our jobs at the SBA and USDA were intensive enough—and still sometimes called for late nights—the sheer number of staff in the agencies made it possible to sneak in a long weekend every once in a while.

While more than half of my large family still resided in Arkansas, only Jude and I lived in Washington and we wouldn't be able to accommodate the 100 or so family members who'd arrive here in July. My father and my son, D.K., would stay with Bob and me; along with two of D.K.'s cousins he had grown up with. They'd been something more like play sisters to him, than mere cousins.

We secured a block of rooms at a Marriott Hotel in Silver Springs—20 miles outside D.C. and a few miles from Jude's home—for the rest of the family.

My family, as we had projected, loved coming to D.C. It had something for everyone—the museums, the malls, the architecture. The children loved riding the Metro. We even visited a distant cousin's church in southwest D.C.—something my father was very happy about. He never felt comfortable traveling and missing church on Sundays.

The reunion was so much fun that some family members stayed on in the area beyond the reunion. While we were ecstatic that it went so well and happy we could host it, we were just as happy to see the last day of the reunion roll around. Not unlike the days when I helped host the event in Arkansas, it was an extraordinary amount of work and built-in stress. I could never thank Bob, Jude and Lorraine enough, for making it all seem so effortless.

There was another event built around the reunion—one that Bob and I had decided needed to take place, just weeks after agreeing to host the reunion. It was a reception announcing our engagement. We'd finally agreed that if we were going to do it, now was as good a time as any. We'd take this opportunity to announce our plans for marriage to our family and friends while they were in the area. And to everyone's astonishment, the wedding was scheduled for December, just six months away.

With the reunion behind us, and fall right around the corner, we quickly turned our attention back to our work and the upcoming wedding. We were both older and more practical about marriages and weddings. We decided that the wedding date would coincide with our

Christmas holiday vacation. We joked that both of our first weddings were planned around other, even more important events.

As fate would have it, however, things didn't happen exactly as planned. Our wedding date was changed twice. It would be years before either Bob or I could laugh about the circumstances surrounding those changes.-

We walked down the aisle as man and wife on December 31, 1994, just days after we'd almost agreed to put the whole thing off. We finally admitted that six months was probably not enough time to plan a wedding. First, we had to agree what kind of wedding it would be. Bob's first marriage had been at the home of a justice of the peace with just him, his bride and the preacher's wife as a witness. I had had a small, rural town's version of a nice church wedding—orchestrated by my mother and the church mothers.

We both would have been fine with a small wedding, but we didn't want to leave out my large family and our extended network of friends who would want to share the special day with us. The wedding planner must have found ours to be the easiest wedding job she'd ever had.

We only met with her once during the six months leading up to the wedding. Our second meeting was during the wedding rehearsal on the eve of our wedding. The caterer for the reception was a friend of my brother, Julius. She contributed an exquisite wedding cake that guests talked about for months after the wedding.

After our New Year's Eve marriage and a Disneyland honeymoon in California, Bob and I returned to D.C. and our jobs at the USDA and the SBA. In addition to catching up on our work, one of the first things on our "to do" list was to find a permanent home that we could call our own.

Our current living quarters had been great for orientating ourselves to the city and settling into our daily routine. Now, two years later, it was time to begin our search for exactly what we wanted in a home. The two years had given us time to take care of some bills from our old lives and begin to save for a mortgage.

Beginning in early April, we would spend our weekends trekking from one end of the city to another. After hearing our complaints, friends suggested our job would be much simpler if we found ourselves a realtor. We did, and for the next couple of months we ran around with the realtor from one end of the city to the other. After three months of nonstop house hunting, we were both weary and prepared to give it a rest.

Bob and I, at the same moment, saw the house that would eventually become our home. We both loved the house's curb appeal and immediately called our realtor to see if we could go inside. He set up a walk-through for the very next day.

The red brick stucco house, built in 1932, was located on Upshur Street in northwest D.C. The sloping front yard was not large, but the backyard made up for it. There was plenty of room for Bob to put his green thumb to good use.

The home was in a racially diverse, upper middle-class neighborhood and included a number of older retirees—mostly former education and government workers. Obviously, there are few neighborhoods in D.C. that don't have their fair share of retired educators and federal workers.

The home wasn't in a trendy neighborhood, but a quiet, settled one. To be honest, Bob initially only liked the house from the street, while I fell madly in love with it lock, stock and barrel right away. We would often half jokingly let it slip that Senator Jay Rockefeller's home was just a few blocks west of ours.

We both loved the fact that the neighborhood was so close to public transportation and to our work. We loved living just 10 minutes from our offices. Neither Bob, nor I wanted to be commuters during our stay in D.C. We wanted the flavor of living in the city.

I'd long believed that homes have souls, or at least personalities. Bob thought I was being silly. Not everyone can sense this, but I sensed a calming spirit and a welcoming personality inside the Upshur home as soon as we walked into it.

No, I don't believe in witches and the bogeyman hiding in closets or attics. But just as we all sense certain karmas in places, I'm convinced that energy—good or bad—remains in the atmosphere of a home, especially if the discord or joy was deep and constant. On the opposite end of the spectrum, I believe happy people and happy relationships leave a good spirit for the next inhabitants.

The Upshur home had been owned by Georgetown University and had been leased or rented out to international faculty and their families over the years. I would have loved to find out more details than I had about the former inhabitants of the home.

We would enjoy five good years in the home at 17th and Upshur. There was a genuine feeling of returning home whenever we traveled, and even when we returned home from work each day. Visiting friends would often comment on the "good karma" emanating from our home.

Bob was an avid gardener, and the sizable backyard allowed him to divert his attention from his work by tilling and planting. While I was never much interested in this type of diversion—especially after spending my childhood working on my father's cotton farm—there was some degree of joy in working with Bob in the backyard flower garden. It was obvious that Bob was the one with the green thumb. I was just having fun and enjoying watching flowers enhance the beauty of our home.

For four of the five years we lived on Upshur, we had one car—my Mitsubishi Galant. Sadly, the D.C. winters had taken its toll on it, and the car was showing its age. Most days Bob and I drove into work together, but rarely returned home at the same time. More often than not, Bob was still at work even at 7 or 8 o'clock in the evening when I left. When the poor Galant began to smoke incessantly, it was relegated to just driving to the grocery store or shopping mall. Bob refused to drive it inside the White House gates.

When the weather was mild, I often walked the two blocks to the corner of 17th and Upshur streets to catch the bus. Unfortunately, most of those mornings, the bus was already filled. I would join the crowd that had to stand during the 20- to 30-minute route to 16th and H streets. It certainly wasn't perfect, but I felt lucky to have this convenient, inexpensive transportation.

My colleagues were always surprised when I mentioned that I rode the city bus, and actually enjoyed these rides. I was, in turn, surprised when they spoke so disparagingly about city transportation and even about the riders. I hadn't realized that in many people's minds, riding a city bus was in the same category as visiting a dentist in the middle of the worst slum area.

Of course, I understood what their attitudes were about. It was different from riding in your own car, with just you taking up your space. In fact, I had had a few experiences that gave me pause. A few times I questioned the sanity and safety of riding public transportation when there were other options.

But this was not always the case. And, besides, this was part of the D.C. experience I wanted to participate in. A natural voyeur of life, I refused to cross public transportation off my list of things to do. In fact, I spent many of those bus rides writing creative stories—memorializing the very situations and people my friends spoke of so disparagingly.

The bus riders included an array of personalities and existences. There were a variety of ethnicities, many of whom only talked to each other and only in their native language. There were a few riders who had obviously taken a lengthy vacation from soap and water, and the constant Bible-toters who offered prayers or read scriptures until their stop was called.

Most visible and most resented, however, were the beggars, especially those perfectly healthy, well-dressed beggars whose English and diction were as perfect as some English professors I've had.

While I understood some of the resentments, I found myself wondering what the homeless beggar must be feeling; having to beg hard-working people for money to eat and live. I wondered how many really did have mental ailments or health problems that the average person couldn't see? How many would actually accept a job or were able to function at a job if one was offered to them?

Arkansas had had only a small homeless community when I left in 1993, and I was caught by surprise when I moved to the U.S. capital and saw the depth and breadth of the homeless problem. They weren't all minorities or old. And you didn't have to ride the city buses and trains to come in contact with them.

The homeless in D.C. could be seen on just about any street—especially in D.C.'s downtown city parks. During winter, they slept on the grates in front of businesses or in bus terminals. There were a few winter deaths each year, though the city made shelters available.

One of the saddest and starkest ironies I witnessed during my time in Washington was the elderly, black woman—obviously homeless—who stood or sat each day outside the entrance to the White House. As we walked into the most important building complex in the country . . . in the world, some might argue . . . there sat this 70- or 80-year-old black woman, every day come rain or shine, or sometimes snow.

The few days each year she missed were during the worst of the winter season. I passed this woman on those days that I rode the bus or train to work. In all those years, I never witnessed her ask anyone for a handout or money. Most times, she stood silently. Other times, she talked only to herself. There were times, however, when her mumbles became clearly, concisely profane, but usually she directed her raucous curses at no one in particular.

A White House civil servant said the woman had perched herself at the 17th Street entrance to the White House 15 years earlier. The rumor was that she had once held an important government position, though no one could recall what position that might have been. The irony was crystal clear, but had the woman started out to make a statement?

As I walked or drove each day to Pennsylvania Avenue, I couldn't help but wonder what impact this decades-long problem had on the quality of all of our lives.

The few dollars I gave to the beggars were literally a drop in the bucket, in contrast to the magnitude of this problem. Giving allowed me to feel more human, at least for a moment, and to assuage my conscience—for I only had to close my eyes to imagine that the man or woman who had slipped between the cracks could be a sister, brother, an old friend or classmate. They might have been productive citizens or loving parents before bad luck or illness transformed them into one of America's invisible human beings we all wish weren't there.

PART V

ALMOST CAMELOT

(1996–1997)

In spite of all I witnessed that was wrong in my new city, it was still a city of magic and wonder. There are two magical seasons in the U.S. capital. One is the cherry blossom season, the opening act for spring in the District of Columbia and the impetus for my falling in love with the city. The other season is just as awe-inspiring, but has a deeper and longer history.

There is absolutely no more spectacular symbolism of Christmas to be found in the world than in our nation's capital, and more specifically, at the White House. Christmastime inside the Beltway transcended political parties, erased the lines down the middle of the aisles and touched those of us who worked every day inside Washington's fishbowls of politics.

This was the one season in which everyone in Washington, at least it seemed, put away the rancor and bitterness that had infiltrated every crevice of our lives during the rest of the year. It was a time of remembering why we were all there.

What most Americans know about our nation's capital is often only what mainstream publications choose to feed us in their front-page stories; or what's selected to air on our 6 o'clock evening news, and even on the fictional television shows depicting the capital city.

Friends and family who visited D.C. during my eight-year stay left amazed and converted. They found a city that was so much more than what had been portrayed—a city made up of real people, many wonderful people, and real communities and families. They were surprised, and probably a little let down, that the city had so much more to offer.

There is homelessness. There is crime. There are drugs. But there is also much more than the shameful crime statistics, the ugly political fights, the rampant scandals, and the sad reports of public school failures.

What is left undisclosed is that the city is an astonishing place to live and to raise children. It is a city filled with venues for learning about the world—the universe, not just our America; and opportunities to contribute to, not just the communities around us, but also a larger community.

What often gave me goose bumps as I walked through these streets or sat at some café or restaurant was the realization that I lived and worked in a place where democracy was born, where the U.S. Constitution—regardless of what many of us view as its oversights—was forged. It is a place where good lawmakers and just leaders make a difference in the lives of the masses by creating, then signing, or not signing a critical bill into law.

It was in the middle of D.C.'s Christmas season that I returned to the White House as presidential diarist—24 months after I'd left to work as communications director at the SBA.

Erskine Bowles, President Clinton's first appointee to head the SBA, was my first boss there. It was under Erskine that the president upgraded the agency to a Cabinet-level department.

Erskine Bowles was a tall, thin, rich businessman from North Carolina with a humorous drawl and a disdain for politics. He had a hug that was warmer than any I'd ever experienced from a grown-up. I was humored by his constant proclamation that he knew nothing about politics, that he was absolutely not a politician, and that he had no business serving in anybody's administration.

Maybe it was because of his loud protestations that Erskine was so loved and respected by both the civil servants and the political appointees at the SBA. More importantly, under his leadership, the agency became better at what it was there to do—serve small businesses. It became more customer friendly, streamlined and efficient. Whatever he lacked in political savvy, Erskine Bowles made up for it in common sense and business savvy.

In late spring, Erskine, who had spent 18 months as head of the SBA, was invited by the president to fill the vacancy of deputy chief of staff to the president. Within days, we had all heard the rumors, but no one knew for certain which rumors to believe. When asked, Erskine feigned ignorance. That was Erskine's way, downplaying his own importance. In fact, Erskine left the SBA in the summer of 1995, right in line with the rumors, to become deputy chief of staff under Leon Panetta.

Phil Lader, a longtime Clinton friend and acquaintance, had served as director of White House personnel and deputy chief of staff and was now moving over to the SBA to take over Erskine's role. He would remain at the agency for roughly 18 months before being appointed ambassador to the United Kingdom. I worked under Phil's leadership for six months, before taking the job as presidential diarist and returning to the White House.

During this time of White House musical chairs, Bob also left the USDA to work at the White House, as director of presidential personnel. He was the fourth and last Clinton appointee to warm the director's seat in the presidential personnel office.

Bob admitted that he'd have to eat his own words that the smartest thing for most appointees was to "get as far away from the White House as possible." No one, though, would ever fault him for going back on his word when the president called.

Though he loved his job at the USDA, Bob's loyalty to President Clinton overrode his desire to stay outside the White House. "How do you say 'No' to the president when he asks you to make a move?" he asked. He would replace a female Atlanta business executive, who resigned and returned to Atlanta.

It was around this time that I learned about a possible presidential diarist position. No one was exactly clear on what the role would entail, but several different people were involved in creating this new role. A sparse job description had been patched together by fall 1995, and even the little I knew convinced me it was a job I wanted.

I was one of a number of people who ended up interviewing for the job that no one was completely sure what it would entail. I was still enjoying my work as public communications director at the SBA at the time. Yet, there was no question that if the job was offered, I would jump at it.

My first interview was in October 1995, with White House Oval Office director Nancy Hernreich. While I was in the running with others vying for the job, I was sure the job fit my background and my love of presidential history perfectly.

My first interview with Nancy was a briefing on what she thought the job entailed and a promise to call me about a subsequent interview. The job fascinated me. I had long held a love and respect for history from my father who taught himself to a great extent and shared all he knew—especially about presidential history—with his children.

My opinionated father would rate each president and tell us why one was better than the other. He would take particular care to explain how black Americans fared under these presidents. The opportunity to take part in presidential history firsthand was very appealing to me.

On my second interview, Nancy and I talked more about the role of the presidential diarist. Before leaving, she handed me a voluminous notebook of information she thought would give me a better understanding of what all this job might involve. She wrote down the names and contact information of two people she had talked with about the position and suggested I call and talk with them.

I called both, later that week, and scheduled dinner with Dorothy Territo, former special assistant to President Johnson; and lunch with John Fawcette, former assistant archivist for Presidential Libraries.

Both of these people were invaluable in my research to learn more about the possibilities for this role. They confirmed Nancy's and others' expectations that this role would be helpful to a more comprehensive presidential history.

Mrs. Territo, who was in her early '70s, was warm, open and filled with anecdotes about her former boss. While she had been President Johnson's secretary, her role had included so much more. She had had the foresight to keep invaluable notes that would serve President Johnson well in his efforts to write his memoirs. That type of insight, Nancy believed, would be important to this new role.

John Fawcette, who had been very instrumental in structuring the presidential collections throughout a number of presidencies, was also extremely helpful. Like Mrs. Territo, he shared wonderful stories about his years of work with presidential archives and how they could be useful.

These voluntary advisers offered invaluable suggestions about what a personal diarist's role would contribute to presidential history, including the opportunity to capture historical moments as they happen. They both suggested that the sooner such a position was in place, the better. The Clinton administration was already into its third year at that time. None of us knew for certain that he'd have a second term.

There was already a presidential diarist position created during the Carter administration under the auspices of the National Archives. Currently, that person was housed in the White House scheduling office. Her role, I learned, was to compile all of the president's daily schedules for the archives and for inclusion later in the presidential libraries documents.

The new role would be considered the personal diarist to the president, Nancy explained, responsible for documenting all aspects of the president's day. While there was no blueprint we had to go by, the role would be a compilation of many different positions and new roles that had never existed before.

Nancy Hernreich was charged with constructing something workable out of all those "maybes." The end result of my conversations with Dorothy and John, and later with presidential historians Doris Kearns Goodwin and Bob Dallek helped confirm that she was going in the right direction. The historians, like Fawcette, were excited that the anecdotal notes not accessible anywhere else in the presidential archives, would be of immense value to future presidential biographers and historians.

Through Mrs. Territo, we also learned that President Johnson had hired an aide toward the end of his tenure to chronicle his presidency. That aide worked closely with Ms. Territo, augmenting her archives with more personal, day-to-day anecdotal information about the president's day. So here were presidential biographers, historians and writers anxiously advising us on how past presidencies had dealt with living history and what a personal diarist to a president could contribute to history.

My third meeting with Nancy was in late November 1995. Afterward, I would view this meeting as our official interview. I had given her a write-up of my meetings with Mrs. Territo and Fawcette and offered my own suggestions and proposals for the position. We talked in detail about those suggestions.

Before leaving her office that day, she told me to expect a call with an answer before the end of the week. A week later, I received her call. She asked if I could stop by her office. By this time, I was still optimistic, but warily so.

I walked out of the northwest gate that day in much the same element I was that first day I'd walked into the White House—with a feeling of watching my life unfold from another plane. I had been offered the one job I had wanted with every fiber of my being. I was happy and grateful beyond words. I realized, again, that amazing, miraculous things continued to happen for me.

I smiled at the guards, as I walked back through the gates. I wondered what their reactions would be if I blurted out: "You'll be seeing a lot of me, now that I'm the president's diarist!" Of course, I'd never have the nerve to do such a thing. Instead, I said a silent, but fervent prayer of gratitude. I pinched myself to confirm I wasn't dreaming. I would continue that dual ritual for the next five years of working inside the White House.

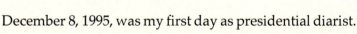

December 8, 1995, was my first day as presidential diarist. It was a typical December day in D.C.—clear, beautiful and cold. The difference between this day and my first stint in the White House almost three years ago was that I was fully cleared, this time.

When I walked through the northwest gate, the blue badge with my name and the White House insignia was awaiting me. The dreaded FBI investigation and federal clearance had been done two years ago, when I went to work at the Small Business Administration. A few months into my new job, however, I was summoned for a second clearance. This one inducted me into the coveted top-secret category required by Oval Office staff.

Nancy Hernreich offered me a welcoming smile as I walked into the outer office of the Oval Office that included her small office and Betty Currie's desk and file area. They both welcomed me back to the White House "to stay this time, we hope," Betty joked.

I smiled and nodded, "Yes, I think I'll stick around this time." There was a comfort in already knowing these two women. I knew Nancy from Arkansas and had met her during her years in the governor's office, where she served as the governor's scheduler for a number of years.

I'd met Betty during the 1992 campaign, and we'd become casual friends during my earlier stint in the White House Media Affairs office.

"I'm assuming you're prepared to give up your personal life, right?" she laughed.

"I guess I am . . . I've heard that's the tradeoff." We all laughed.

Nancy offered to show me around—which turned out to be a short walk down the West Wing hall. We walked past the Roosevelt Room, directly across from the empty Oval Office. "He's traveling this morning," Nancy offered as I looked toward the door.

George Stephanopoulos stood talking with his assistant. He smiled and nodded as we passed. I didn't know it then, but George wouldn't remain much longer at the White House. Two doors farther down the hall, Nancy stopped inside the doorway of a large room partitioned into three office spaces and a secretary's desk.

"Here we are. This is where you'll be stationed, Janis. If you want, you can put your stuff there, and I'll introduce you to some of our other Oval Office staff."

My office space was the front cubicle nearest the door. I'd later learn that Pat Buchanan had resided in this very space during the Reagan administration. One aide joked, "at least you can say you're three doors down from the Oval Office. You don't have to tell them it's just a desk in a corner."

My suite mates included Rebecca, Nancy's assistant, who was in her early 20s, and Stephen, a Texan who was in his late 20s and who served as the president's personal assistant. Over time, I'd join the rest of the White House aides who affectionately referred to Stephen as "POTUS' butt-boy."

Though I'd worked in the Old Executive Office Building directly across the walkway, I'd forgotten how different in size and ambience the offices were. The OEOB's offices were spacious with oversized windows and lighting. The West Wing offices, by and large, were less than half that size.

While most West Wing offices had no windows and little ambience, the difference, I'd learned, was like having an office in Manhattan and one in the Bronx.

"Location, location, location," Stephen had jokingly told me that first week. "Take my word for it, Janis, there are staff members who would pay you part of their salary to get an office—even a cubicle like ours—in the West Wing."

The tall, attractive young woman with the huge smile turned out to be someone I knew. Pam had been Erskine Bowle's executive assistant at SBA and now she was his executive assistant at the White House. It was wonderful to see her friendly smile and to hear her familiar North Carolina drawl I'd grown accustomed to at SBA.

"Hey, Janis, I heard you were coming. It's great to be working with you again." We hugged each other only as Southerners do, so comfortably.

"Is Erskine here?" I asked, excited that I might be able to say hello. Pam shook her head and said he was out at a meeting.

"Well, I'll say hello later." When I saw him the next day, he still had the most genuine laughter and hug of any politician I'd ever met. His Southern charm, as usual, was turned on "high" as he gave me a generous North Carolina bear hug.

"What you doin', girl . . . followin' me?" Erskine drawled.

"Yep. You didn't think I was going to stay at SBA with you gone, did you?" We chatted for a while before he was called up front. He gave me a knowing look and said, "Got to go see the boss."

In those early days, there was a lot of guessing by a large number of White House staff who really didn't know what I was doing there. I knew several of the senior aides were well aware of what my role entailed. It was one of those open secrets that no one discussed, and I was encouraged not to offer any explanations. This, however, allowed staff to create their own ideas about exactly what I was up to.

It made sense that my title was something less ostentatious than personal diarist to the president. So my official title on paper was special assistant to the president and records manager. Before we left the White House, it was changed to special adviser for presidential history.

The sticky part would be separating my role from Ellen McCatharan, the civil servant who became the presidential diarist during the Carter administration. There was no question that her role served an important purpose, but early on, the question of whether the two jobs could be combined was a topic of discussion. In the end, I think the decision was that they couldn't.

Ellen was responsible for collecting and dissecting the presidential records and cataloguing them for the national archives. My role was documenting living history as it happened, from observations and collections of personal documents; maintaining a diary that included a more in-depth, more personalized chronicle of the president's day.

Ellen and I got to know each other quite well during my five years at the White House. We, in fact, spent a great deal of time comparing notes in efforts to determine how our jobs might be better coordinated.

I returned to the White House just as the Christmas season was coming into full bloom in the city. How fitting for someone who had always believed in the miraculous powers of Christmas, someone whose southeast Arkansas childhood was colored by that magical time.

I can't imagine a more meaningful Christmas gift in 1995 than being offered the role of presidential diarist. It was during this season that my memories of growing up on Varner Road often came alive again, inside my mind. I thought about how, for years as a child, I'd convinced myself that I would get that red bicycle or the pink bed with curtains I'd seen in the J.C. Penney catalog. Though neither ever showed up under my Christmas tree on Varner Road, that fact never stopped me from believing or dreaming. And I never stopped loving this special holiday.

As I grew older and a little wiser, I realized that Santa's midnight visits were dictated by Daddy's cotton crop that year. Even during the worst of crop years, we could always count on our individual Christmas boxes filled with nuts, and candy and fireworks and fruit. And, maybe, maybe . . . if Daddy had a good crop that year, a small toy worth so much more in our hearts than it did to the man at the Pine Bluff discount store who sold it to Daddy.

Part of the allure of Christmas, though, had little to do with the gifts we received, but the sights and smells and sounds of Christmastime, the pungent smells of the red mesh bags stuffed with fresh fruit from Professor King each year; the bright blues and reds and yellows of the lights that hung from our fir tree days before and after Christmas Day.

And, those wonderful, memorable Christmas dinners—the turkey and ham and hog sausages and cakes and pies and home-made rolls . . . smells that would fill our home for days to come, and stayed with us even into our dreams.

Though our impoverished reality never quite matched what my childish dreams created, there was surely something to our ability to conjure up fantasies so much more expansive than the children who had something a lot closer to a perfect Christmas.

In 1995, I was struck by what seemed almost like a reincarnation of my childhood dreams of what Christmas could be like . . . what it must be like for the luckiest children in the world.

Nothing belies the myths about D.C. more than the Christmas holiday in our nation's capital. The holiday brings a magnificent, magical makeover for this already beautiful city.

Like most cities, the holiday always begins in earnest during the Thanksgiving weekend, and it doesn't end until well after Christmas Day. The transformation is helped along by the carefully decorated store windows up and down the main thoroughfares of Georgetown, downtown D.C., and the outlying malls in D.C., Virginia and Maryland.

The spirit of Christmas seemed never-ending—an arresting, giant Christmas card from one end of the city to the other. A December walk or drive through the city offers a smorgasbord in home decorations from beautiful, but demure candles or lightings to giant decorated pines and Christmas wreaths to fit every persuasion, including some with endless, colorful, sparkling lights and decorative bows.

Back in the downtown area, holiday music made us know that it was the Christmas season. It was piped into stores and restaurants day and night—music that soothed the senses and awakened our memories of Christmases past

The White House has a long, rich tradition of celebrating Christmas in a big way. And for most presidents and their wives, a highlight of the season is finding ways to share the celebrations with the public.

Had I not walked through the East Wing as the workers strung the decorations, hauled in the giant trees and carted in boxes and boxes of ornaments, I could almost believe that Santa's elves did indeed stop by to leave a bit of magic in the most popular house in the world.

The ambience was a child's dream of a perfect Christmas. The larger-than-life trees with hand-made decorations from every part of the world, the pungent smells of Christmas firs, and the angelic voices of children from the local choirs brought in to serenade the nightly visitors to the residence.

I admit now that I found excuses to walk through the residence during my workdays. The child inside me leapt with joy and wonder, still, at the beauty created within the place I now worked each day.

President and Mrs. Clinton were magnanimous in opening their White House and residence to visitors and guests during the holiday seasons. They would never have guessed that one of their aides would be so moved by the magical Christmas ambience created at 1600 Pennsylvania Avenue.

Yet, while I was privileged to enjoy the wonder and beauty within those walls, it was difficult not to remember there were so many families for whom Christmas was simply another day, another sad day in their lives. I saw these families every day, during my lunchtime walks, and in the morning as I jaunted from the bus stop.

This amazing city—my new home—was a perfect symbol of paucity and power. As much as I tried, I couldn't forget the faces of the children who sat with their mothers begging for tokens, for food. I couldn't forget what I knew . . . that there were many in this wonderful city that had no sense of this kind of Christmas. There were so many whose Christmases fell far short of being merry, or pretty, or magical.

I couldn't erase the thought when I went home at night that, at least for a time, I was a part of a privileged few, surrounded by power and riches, while blocks away men and women and children hovered in the cold or squeezed into overcrowded shelters. I was warm and protected within this city of staggering crime and poverty statistics.

The president and Mrs. Clinton hosted two weeks of holiday receptions inviting congressional leaders, Cabinet members, administration appointees, White House staff and all their families. The tiered parties ended with long lines of guests waiting for their turn to greet and take photos with the president, Mrs. Clinton and Chelsea.

I knew I would be going home to spend Christmas with my own family in Arkansas. I would take a small piece of this celebration in the form of Christmas ornaments for my family and friends.

Bob and I shopped in the White House store for unique souvenirs we'd share with friends who might never have an opportunity to visit this place. The Christmas season at the White House reminded me of all I had to be thankful for, of the miracles that still abound in spite of the good and bad that went on in the world. It forced me to pray for peace and goodwill and the softening of hearts, that *all* Americans would, indeed, be included in the spoils and riches.

By January 1996, most White House staffers were back from their Christmas vacations and settling back into work days at the White House. It didn't take long to wrap ourselves back into what we were faced with each day and close our eyes to the rest of the world. Though President Clinton made known his policy of aides spending time with their families, you wouldn't know it by the hours he worked past quitting time.

The Clintons did take holiday vacations, leaving the White House in the hands of capable managers and senior administrators for a short time. The chiefs of staff were responsible for keeping the engine running while the "boss" was away. As they had for many years before he became president, the Clintons spent the last part of their vacation at Phil Lader's annual Renaissance Weekend in North Carolina.

Shortly after his return to the White House in January, the president learned that former Texas congresswoman Barbara Jordan—the only black U.S. lawmaker from Texas for many years—had passed away. His advisers desperately hoped he'd send a surrogate and remain at the White House to prepare for his State of the Union speech. The president would not only attend the funeral service, but deliver a eulogy, as well.

By all accounts, President Clinton attended and eulogized funerals of more administration officials, family and close friends than any president before him. There might have been at least two good reasons for this: the president had far more friends than most people, and his oratory skills and gift for saying just the right thing at the right time were as much a part of the requests for his eulogies as were his place in the Oval Office.

It made perfect sense that on January 20, 1996, President Clinton would deliver the eulogy at the funeral of Barbara Jordan, one of the greatest orators and political giants in Texas. Joining the president in Houston were former Texas Governor Ann Richardson, Mayor Bob Lanier and Representative Barbara Lee. A vocalist sang the congresswoman's favorite song, "This Little Light of Mine."

In his eulogy, President Clinton said the last time he'd seen Barbara Jordan was in late fall "when Liz Carpenter talked me into giving a speech on race relations during the Million Man March. I walked out into that vast arena. There were 17,000 people, but I could only see one—Barbara Jordan, smiling at me."

He recalled that the former congresswoman had given an eloquent keynote address at the 1992 presidential convention" and in 1994, he had given her the Presidential Medal of Freedom. "I noticed her wearing it today, and it touches me so to know that she is now going to a place where her reward will be greater," the president said.

According to his aides, Clinton shared more touching and funny stories with his Cabinet members and staff on his way home from the funeral.

In the few days before delivering his third State of the Union address, the president spent part of his days reviewing and rewriting the speechwriters' drafts. It was both a subject of humor and despair for the hardworking speechwriters that rarely would their speeches be left with any semblance of the words they started out with.

Those who knew him best swore the president only used speechwriters to get him to thinking. With that very necessary push, he would do the real work of writing his own speeches.

As was the custom for State of the Union speeches, the president met first with his speechwriters and a few writers from outside. Then he met with the speechwriters, the communications director and staff, some Cabinet members and other senior staff in the theatre for two days of serious rehearsal with the teleprompter.

Nothing inspired me as much during my White House days as the privilege of being a part of this group who watched this process from beginning to end. The president was at once funny, irate, mimicking, impressive and almost always compassionate about issues that had to do with everyday people. The light moments were balanced by moments of deep seriousness.

Any changes he made always made his speeches better. No one, not even his brilliant speechwriters, were better at saying just exactly what needed to be said. It was absolutely fascinating to watch the work involved in the speeches that went down in history, as sentence by sentence, page by page, his advisers helped him frame his appeal to the American people—the words that would boost America's confidence, convince them they had chosen the right leader and that we were indeed, moving the country in the right direction.

Four months after beginning my new job at the White House, I received an envelope in the mail that meant just one thing—jury duty. What timing. At 43 years old and a temporary resident of the District of Columbia, Uncle Sam decided now was a good time to call me for jury duty for the first time in my life.

After sitting for half a day in the jury pool of 50 people, I was sure I wouldn't be one of the people picked from the pool. I was wrong. In spite of the irritation I knew better than to express, I was forced to chuckle as I left the courthouse that day. What would Daddy think about my being picked as a juror in a D.C. court case as benign as a suit between real estate companies ... nothing provocative like a murder, rape, or drug case—Daddy's preconceived notions of the only things that happened in this city?

I immediately went to Nancy's office to share with her my predicament.

"That's not the worst part," I said, wincing. "The judge told us to prepare for two weeks of jury duty, at least."

No one could believe my bad luck, including me. I would listen to two weeks of testimony from white-collar criminals suing each other over a bad business deal. I was encouraged not to make a big deal out of it all.

Just into my second week on the jury, I was sure I'd learned more about Washington's lucrative real estate business than I thought I'd ever need. It was a few days before the closing arguments, on April 3rd, that I walked out of the courthouse for lunch and saw a message on my pager. It was Betty Currie's number. I quickly went to the courthouse phone and called. I was sure Nancy asked her to call and ask me to stop by the office that evening.

"Ron Brown's plane just went down in the mountains of Croatia. That's all we know. I'll let you know what we learn."

I stopped breathing for a moment, certain I hadn't heard Betty correctly. "Betty, what did you say?" I didn't want to believe I'd heard her correctly.

"Ron Brown was on a trade mission in Croatia, and his plane has disappeared. We're waiting to hear something more."

I shook my head in disbelief as the phone clicked. Suddenly I remembered that my brother Jude often traveled with the Secretary of Commerce. Jude was assistant secretary for International Trade and might very well be on the Secretary's plane. My heart stopped. There was no way I could go back into the courtroom before learning the whereabouts of my brother. I called Betty back to see if she had a roster of people on the plane.

"No . . . not yet. We're waiting for the list now."

I told her I needed to know if Jude was on that list. I heard her intake of breath. She knew Jude well. They liked each other a lot. While I waited for her to call, I checked to make sure the session hadn't resumed. I dialed Jude's office number, but wasn't able to locate him or his assistant. I imagined the whole department must be either numb or going crazy. Most of the phones throughout the department were likely going unanswered.

Finally, it dawned on me that Lorraine, Jude's wife, might be home. She was. Jude was not traveling with Secretary Brown. I hurriedly asked Lorraine if she'd heard about the plane crash. She hadn't and became immediately fraught with worry.

"I have to hang up, Janis. I need to locate Jude, and find out what's going on." We said our goodbyes, and I was grateful, but still worried.

I was anxious that evening to hurry to the White House. I prayed under my breath as I caught the train that would take me to 17th and Pennsylvania, two blocks from the White House. I arrived in the West Wing in time to see a White House in turmoil.

At 1 p.m. that afternoon, Croatian President Franjo Tudjman had called President Clinton to confirm that Secretary Brown's plane had been found and identified. Everyone aboard had died in the crash in the Croatian mountains. There were 33 passengers and crew, including Ron Brown's personal staff, military officials and a trade mission—businessmen and women from all walks of life.

The president, Mrs. Clinton and one of the president's highest-ranking White House aides, Alexis Herman, traveled by motorcade to Ron Brown's home and visited with his wife, Alma, and the rest of the Brown family. Afterward, the president went to the Commerce Department and spoke to the 700-plus staff and employees, promising them, as he had Alma Brown, that he would protect the Commerce Department Secretary's legacy.

President Clinton and Ron Brown had been more than mere political allies after the 1992 election. Bill Clinton had been awed by the 54-year-old man's political genius and his gift for networking. Ron Brown had brilliantly guided the candidates through an exciting New York convention. He was seen in many political circles as the consummate rainmaker in all things political. Bill Clinton had thanked him for a job well done by appointing him head of the U.S. Department of Commerce. Ron was the first black man to hold that position.

At 12:15 p.m., on Wednesday, April 10, 1996, President and Mrs. Clinton, his entire Cabinet and most White House senior aides, along with thousands of Commerce Department employees and people from around the country—Americans of all persuasions, black, white, Hispanic, Asian and others—gathered at the Cathedral Church of Saint Peter and Saint Paul, to grieve Ronald H. Brown's passing and his family's loss.

Alma Brown and her children's faces would become household images, and the service would be widely reported on for days. It was an amazing outpouring of love for a man who everyone called Ron. Those who knew him remembered his expansive personality and optimism.

The Howard University Choir sang a rendition of Ron Brown's favorite spirituals and one of President Clinton's, "His Eyes Are on the Sparrow."

Black Entertainment Television's Robert Johnson read an excerpt from "Ulysses," by Alfred, Lord Tennyson. George Fisher, CEO of the Kodak Company, did a second reading of Ecclesiastics 39: 1, 6-10. Michael Brown, Ron's beloved son, spoke eloquently. Wynton Marsalis offered a musical elegy—"Flee as the Bird to the Mountain." And Ron Brown's longtime friend and colleague, Alexis Herman, gave a eulogy.

President Clinton's eulogy for Ron Brown was what many in the quiet, crowded sanctuary awaited. His somber, heart-wrenching homage to the man he called a friend touched the emotional chords of all who were inside the cathedral and those who watched from around the world.

It would be weeks before the White House would return to normalcy. Ron Brown's death left a pall over the Clinton administration. It dampened the spirit of the good work being done for the American people because all inside the White House, including President Clinton, felt the loss of a stalwart leader in that work.

President Clinton had been badgering friends and anyone else who would listen to him with discussions about how to fix the race problems in our country for as long as anyone who knew him could remember.

He hadn't just jumped on the civil rights train once he set foot in Washington. He had been compassionate and angry about America's racial divide all of his life—at least as long as he'd been old enough to understand it. As a politician, he'd talked about it openly and frankly—from Arkansas to Africa. And to hear political pundits accuse him of using the race conversation as a political ploy was as funny as it was ludicrous. They didn't know the man, at all.

By the time the president had brought together a group of people to help him think through what a race initiative might look like, he was already receiving friendly advice from good Democrats about what such an effort might mean politically.

There were a slew of good people inside and outside the White House advising President Clinton on what direction to go with his One America Race Initiative. At least some of the whispering heard during that time was, "I can't believe he's doing this."

It depended on who was saying it, as to how it came out. There were his loyalists and proponents of continued discussion about civil rights who wondered what took so long. On the other side of the fence, there were those who walked a straight line down the middle who thought the president was rocking the boat when he really didn't have to rock it at all. There were bigger political fish to fry.

The president was scheduled to announce the Race Initiative during his commencement speech at the University of California in San Diego. If the air on the flight out to San Diego and later in work sessions were any indication, there was a divide, right inside his own White House. Certainly, there were raw nerves being rubbed the wrong way.

The speechwriters didn't all agree on what was acceptable language. Neither did the senior advisers. In the end, the president's speech about race and relations could have been meant for the many people who believed they were open and inclusive because their openness and inclusiveness had never been tested.

Many of his staunchest advocates believed he was biting off more than he could chew, opening up a Pandora's box of trouble that ran deeper than most people wanted to go. There was an undercurrent of divide between the white and black advisers. Those black aides who traveled to D.C. with him from Arkansas believed this was a cause he truly owned, a strength that would embolden his presidency and his integrity as a leader.

More recent advisers who got to know him through the campaign believed he was painting himself into a corner as a bleeding heart liberal, and nothing else he did would be given credit. They believed the Race Initiative might serve as a stumbling block, an Achilles' heel that would give rabid Republicans the ammunition they needed to sway undecided voters away from a second Clinton term.

Was it a courageous step? Absolutely. Was it politically astute on the eve of an election year? Many believed not. Every president had danced around the race issue since Lyndon Johnson, who was actually honest enough to admit he did not go meekly into the civil rights arena.

Once Kennedy left Johnson holding the civil rights bag, and Martin Luther King Jr. and others prodded him toward the right path, Johnson took up the equality and fairness helm with unexpected gusto. Unlike any president—Southern or otherwise—in American history, he stood up to the segregationists and conservatives on the side of fairness.

Unfortunately, it was not Johnson's courage on this issue, but the country's dissatisfaction with his position on the Vietnam War that would leave a blot on his political legacy. But, his courage on the civil rights issue would also contribute greatly to his political downfall and the weakening of the Democratic Party for years to come.

That was the unspoken fear clouding Bill Clinton's desire to make a statement about righting this centuries-old wrong. The issue put him squarely between a rock and a hard place. Blacks and liberal Democrats said he was playing it safe since claiming the White House. Some accused him, in fact, of teetering on the edge of the right of center. It was these groups that prodded him toward this courageous stance on race.

The conservative Democrats, however, thought he was being foolish, playing loose politics, trying to do too much in one term. There was a fear that this would kill the party's chances at maintaining the house and the presidency for another term.

There weren't many politicians or others who believed any earth-shaking changes would come about in light of the initiative; it was just the impression that he was using his bully pulpit to speak out about an issue that would always rub someone the wrong way. It didn't matter that the president insisted this was an effort to get Americans talking to each other, "not at each other."

In June 1996, President Clinton stood on the stage of the San Diego State University in La Jolla, California, dressed in the ceremonious black commencement garb. Included in his commencement address to graduating seniors and their families, was his introduction of his One America Race Initiative.

He pointed to his Filipino-born White House doctor, Connie Mariano, as "a shining example of excellence rooted in the many backgrounds that make up this great country." Thus, his One America Race Initiative now pointed to more than just blacks or whites, and was suddenly made more palatable for those who feared its divisiveness.

The Clinton White House was at the height of the one most exciting season inside the Beltway, the presidential election season. It was in the air and touched everything in our lives. We were all read the riot act: No intermingling politics with our jobs—or to a certain extent our policies. But we also knew this was a very fine line to tow.

There was no question that what we did to change the lives of everyday people and how well we let the public know what we were doing would have an impact on whether Bill Clinton was re-elected, becoming the first two-termed Democratic president since President Franklin Roosevelt.

No matter how hard we tried we couldn't ignore that high-pitched political fever that comes along with presidential campaigns. Though the president's Republican opponent was the stately—if not very exciting—Bob Dole, it was looking more and more as if Bill Clinton would be a two-term president. His political pollsters whispered their optimism loud enough for us to hear, while making sure they kept mum outside the White House and certainly around the opponent's team.

The president had spent months of almost sleepless nights, breaking every fundraising record in the Democratic Party's history. The regular gatherings in the White House of political leaders and business constituents, dubbed "coffees," were as successful as they were controversial, thanks to a fanning of the political fires in the waning days of the campaign.

The most exciting discussions around the White House late that summer concerned the president's trip to Chicago aboard a 13-car train dubbed the 21st Century Express. Given all the maneuvering by staff and others to get on board, one might have thought the train was going all the way to Paris. The 21st Century Express was the place to be when the train pulled out of Huntington, West Virginia, that August.

The president and Mrs. Clinton previewed a video produced by the Democratic National Committee just hours before departing on the four-day train ride from West Virginia to Chicago. This was a historical train trip and a historical occasion—for the second time, Bill Clinton would accept his party's nomination as president of the United States.

Of course, such an event resulted in a discussion between Nancy and me as to whether I would travel with the president on this trip. Clearly, how expansive my role would be was something of a balancing act for Nancy, too. She tried to be fair without overstepping our boundaries. The balance was how to allow me access without stirring up too much interest or problems later.

Thus, I tried never to be overly demanding about what I thought my role required. I was hopeful, however, that Nancy would see this trip as one with an obvious historical value—and politically safe enough for my travel with the president. The president's personal aides always traveled with him, and the documents they collected, as well as stories, were great addendums to my daily diary of the president's days. I hoped, however, that I'd be able to gain firsthand knowledge during this trip. I was pleasantly surprised when Nancy agreed.

There was a strange excitement about the train trip for me. Yes, it had much to do with Bill Clinton's pending re-election, but just as much to do with being inside a bubble of history, knowing the link this trip represented to past presidential campaigns as far back as Abraham Lincoln. It was a great honor for me to take part in this recreation of that history in 1996.

The 21st Century Express departed Huntington in the early afternoon on Sunday, August 25th. I could have been wrong, but President Clinton's face showed as much excitement as any of his staff, as he waved to the large crowd who had come to the Huntington train station to bid him "good travels." Some would meet us in Chicago at the Democratic Convention.

As an assistant to the president, Bob was pretty much of a natural to travel with the president to Chicago. While this was one of the few presidential trips in which we traveled together, Bob didn't see it in quite the light I did. In fact, he was probably one of less than a handful of people in the White House who would not feel left out, if he never traveled during a presidential trip.

A young White House aide once called Bob's office very excited that he could invite Bob on a trip to Arkansas with the president. Bob apologetically told the young aide, he couldn't go, adding, "You know, Bill Clinton and I have traveled every back road in Arkansas . . . and a few outside Arkansas. And while I would love to travel on AF1 to Arkansas with him, I can't. He'll understand if you tell him I'm stuck in my office, working hard on his personnel priorities."

We both were happy to be traveling with Bill Clinton on this particular day on our way to the 21st century. I wondered if President Kennedy, who had made a train stop in this very city 37 years earlier, thought about what America and the world might be like in the 21st century?

The list of passengers was an impressive one. Democratic leaders, politicians, friends and staff joined the president. The train's very first whistle-stop was

Ashland, Kentucky, where country western star Billy Ray Cyrus wowed the passengers and the huge crowd waiting in the summer heat for President Clinton's arrival. Bill Clinton would be the first president to visit Ashland since 1972 when President Richard Nixon visited the town.

Billy Ray Cyrus first sang a heart-rending version of the national anthem, then serenaded President Clinton with an original song written in honor of his presidency and his pending re-election.

The next stop was Chillicothe, Ohio, a town I never knew existed. But there were plenty of people there to prove it did, indeed, exist. There were more than 16,000 overexcited Ohioans yelling, screaming, waving flags and banners as the 21st Century Express pulled to a stop. Senator John Glenn, still prepossessing at 70 years old, spoke briefly to the audience, then hopped aboard the train to travel to Chicago with President Clinton.

At a stop in Columbus, Ohio, civil rights icon Rosa Parks was in the crowd. She and President Clinton talked, as the photojournalists had a heyday with shots from every angle. CBS News anchorwoman Paula Zahn began her prescheduled interview with the president, an interview that wouldn't end until we came to our final stop.

In Arlington, Ohio, an elderly woman told the president she had been around when President Harry S. Truman traveled the same train route 48 years earlier. President Clinton rode the 2 millionth Jeep as it rolled off the local Jeep plant's assembly line. The crowd of 25,000 people was in awe of seeing a president, used to being chauffeured around in limousines, enjoying his brief jaunt in the Jeep.

President Franklin Roosevelt had rode through Wynadotte, Michigan, during his campaign, but President Clinton's stop would mark the first official visit of a sitting president. And, likely, Mr. Roosevelt's ride through the town didn't garner a crowd of 15,000.

The crowd gathered at the Bacon Memorial District Library to listen as young Justin Whitney and Nicole Rushman read "The Little Engine That Could" in honor of Mrs. Clinton and Chelsea. They were told that Mrs. Clinton had read the book to Chelsea as a child, and it was still their favorite children's book.

A worthy quid pro quo to Justin and Nicole's reading was President Clinton's announcement that effective that day, a $2.5 billion national literacy program would be implemented nationwide through his new AmeriCorps program.

His stop in Battle Creek, Michigan, was the first presidential visit since Lyndon Johnson's visit in 1965. But it was the first presidential train stop since President William H. Taft's train visit in 1918.

In Battle Creek, the president was met by his childhood babysitter, 96-year-old Eartha Clay, who was born in Forrest City, Arkansas. Mrs. Clay told reporters she had worked on the farm of James Eldridge—Bill Clinton's grandfather—in Hope, Arkansas. She had also cared for young Billy Blythe (Clinton's childhood name) while his grandparents worked.

Mrs. Clay and her late husband had worked for President Franklin Roosevelt's New Works Program, chartering buses to take workers all over the country to work in factories. They had both continued working for the president until his death in 1945.

Clay enjoyed the attention of the White House reporters, telling them, "I was the first one to vote for him (Roosevelt), and I got a lot of other people here to vote for him, too." She was proud to say she had babysat for one great president and worked closely with another.

By the time President Clinton made it to Kalamazoo, Michigan, where a presidential candidate by the name of Abraham Lincoln had visited 140 years earlier, it was in the middle of an extremely hot day. So hot, in fact, that four people in the crowd of 5,000 fainted, including the sign language interpreter.

Sweat poured from the president's face, and his shirt was plastered to his body. His voice had become a hoarse rasp from the heat outside and the air-conditioned train. He continued to speak, though, pausing only when another audience member fainted from the heat. And then only long enough to direct his medical staff to assist the heat victims. Once he was sure they would be fine, he resumed his raspy voiced speech.

Bill Clinton's last train stop was Michigan City, Indiana. He was proud to say he was the first president to stop in Michigan City in 97 years. After a rousing speech to 10,000 people— many of whom were students—he flew on to Chicago, where he would meet Mrs. Clinton. They would remain at Chicago's Sheraton Hotel for the next two nights.

Bob and I were part of the president's entourage bringing up the rear of the train ride. We arrived in Chicago later. We were as exhausted as we were exhilarated. Gratefully, convention volunteers in golf carts arrived on the spot to deposit us at the front lobby of the

Sheraton, as well. After the four-day whirlwind train tour of Middle America, a hot shower, some rest and sleep were the priorities on just about everyone's mind that night.

Almost Camelot (1996–1997)

August 29, 1996

Hey Daddy,

 Guess where I am? Chicago . . . your kind of town! In Chicago, remembering all the stories you told us about the years you spent here, working in the restaurants and helping to build Union Station? I still tell people about how you remember spitting and watching it roll down the street like a marble! Thank goodness, we're here in August. But we are staying at a hotel not far from Union Station.

 The president accepted the nomination tonight, and I already know you were sitting in the living room watching it as it all happened. I know you are as happy and proud as we are.

 Honestly, sometimes I wonder why in the world he would want another term, the way the Republicans tried to destroy him the past four years? But what president is going to give up a chance to be president a second time? We're all lucky that he's not letting them run him home.

 This first term taught us how scared power brokers are of change—and how far they will go to keep things the same. I think a lot of people here are afraid that he's trying to turn the status quo upside down—not simply trying to open America up to all of its citizens, not just the "haves" and the already privileged. We know that's what he's about and always has been.

The train ride was really something! The look of hope and excitement on the hundreds of thousands of faces was so invigorating for someone who is part of this presidency. You could tell this was a once-in-a-lifetime experience for most of them.

I met Rosa Parks at one stop and told her that Daisy Bates was my friend and my mentor. She had lots of good things to say about Daisy. The astronaut, Senator John Glenn, rode the train all the way to Chicago. And in Battle Creek, Michigan, I met one of the president's childhood babysitters, who worked for President Roosevelt, too!

These last four years have made me realize more than ever that, in spite of everything still wrong with America, it is an amazing country. When people tell me Bill Clinton has forgotten the people who got him elected, I want to tell them, he's a president, not a king . . . presidents aren't all-powerful. People outside D.C. seem not to realize that Congress holds a great deal of power and deserves a lot of the blame for things they complain about not getting done.

I think Bill Clinton is able to fill people with so much hope that they just expect him to get it all done—without help from anyone, including Congress. They don't know politicians are only as good as their last election. Unfortunately, he has to play the political games just like every other president has—especially if he wants to get re-elected. Then, maybe he'll be able to make some of those changes people want.

He's taking a lot of criticism on his welfare reform policy. I can imagine you have a few concerns, too. I admit my emotions are mixed. How can I forget that we depended on welfare for a time? We probably couldn't have made it without it. So, how could I ever go along with doing away with welfare assistance? I think most minorities see it the same way, even if they never personally benefited.

But I really don't think that's what the president's policy is calling for. He isn't saying do away with it—just make it better and more efficient so that it meets people's real needs. People need to use it when they have no other options, then once they're on their feet, move on . . . especially the young, healthy people who can be trained or retrained for jobs.

I really think this plan is a good one . . . if it works. The problem is, we have to depend on individual states to make it work. I don't envy him having to go before angry leaders who see the bill as him caving in to the Republicans who have always been negative about programs for the poor. The bad thing about political leaders with good hearts is that politics sometimes get in the way of the good they want to do.

Anyway, I've done enough preaching to the choir. Cross your fingers . . . Bob and I will either be back in Little Rock come January or settling here in D.C. for four more years. I have to run. Take care of yourself, Daddy . . . and take everybody in Gould to those voting polls!

Love,
Faye

It was November 4, 1996, the eve of Election Day. After a stop in Manchester, New Hampshire, the president moved on to Sioux Falls, Dakota. Sioux Falls was the president's absolute last campaign stop before flying to Little Rock, for what we all believed would be a victory for the president, his speech, and nonstop celebrations.

He worked an endless rope line past midnight, shaking hands, seemingly, with the full population of the city. Before leaving, he bounded up on the stage with Jerry Jeff Walker and sang, "This Land is Your Land," along with the band and the crowd.

Air Force One was loaded with buckets of Mango ice cream and bottles of champagne. Macarena music blared throughout the president's plane in anticipation of Mrs. Clinton's promised Macarena dance with Vice President Gore, upon her husband's re-election.

Everyone except Bill Clinton seemed exhausted. He was ready to grab the brass rings, this last time. Almost 1,000 people were there to greet him when he arrived in Little Rock that night. He couldn't just wave and walk to the limousine, of course. He shook hands with hundreds of people, including old friends and loyalists.

There were more than 300 White House staffers, Cabinet members, Democratic National Committee officials and Democratic Senate and House leaders who boarded chartered planes that would take us all to Little Rock. The city was just getting over that first hullabaloo back in November 1992. But Arkansas had grown up a lot since then. The state was far more prepared this time for this kind of celebration and even having the eyes of the world focused on Arkansas.

The Clinton family stayed at the Excelsior Hotel in downtown Little Rock. Bill Clinton would give one of two speeches from the hotel on election night. His election watch party would be there and, if everything went as expected, the victory party would be held there, too. The next morning, he'd reunite with hundreds of former members of his governor's staff.

As the president, Mrs. Clinton and Chelsea went together to vote at Union Station, the rest of the world continued to turn on its axis that Election Day. A small New Hampshire hamlet called Dixieville had continued its 30-year tradition: the 28 residents of the town had already allocated their presidential votes—18 went to Bob Dole; eight went to Bill Clinton; and one each went to Harry Browne, the Libertarian candidate, and Ross Perot, the Independent candidate.

It was a different Election Day than the one four years ago. We were different, too—not just older, but more confident in our president and wiser about the good and the bad side of running a country.

One thing hadn't changed for the hundreds of thousands of people thronging the streets of central Arkansas on Election Day—the most powerful Arkansan, and American, was still our own Bill Clinton. That night we expected to celebrate . . . but not yet. Not until every poll was closed, and the commentator called a clear victory . . . again, for William Jefferson Clinton.

It was a balmy November evening in Little Rock as we all pretended we were nervous about who would win the election. As if we didn't know that he would make another of his rousing, hopeful, poignant acceptance speeches later that night . . . or that he would join Hillary and Chelsea as they made their rounds thanking supporters and accepting congratulations from all.

The small, but growing city of Little Rock was a picture postcard of all Bill Clinton preached. Blacks and whites, and a sprinkling of others, made up a vibrant, happy throng of celebrants up and down the main streets of Little Rock. Those who weren't celebrating stayed inside their doors or languished on the sidelines looking on.

Markham Street was the "Main Street" of Little Rock on Election night. All of the action would take place at the Excelsior Hotel and then at the beautiful Old State House next door. Celebrities were at the Excelsior and Capitol hotels. No one would dare ask the street celebrants to "hold it down" . . . they, too, were celebrating four more years of our native son's presidency.

Shortly before midnight, the decision was clear: our own Bill Clinton had done it again. He made history by being the first Democratic president to win two terms since Franklin Roosevelt. Bill Clinton had handily won re-election against Republican Senator Bob Dole of Kansas.

Though the country might still see Arkansas as small town, America, we Arkansans now knew how to put on a presidential-style celebration—it was our Bill Clinton being feted after all. Award-winning opera singer Jessye Norman sang "America," "Amazing Grace," and "God Bless America" at the Old State House before the Clintons and Gores came out.

As tradition demands, one of Bill Clinton's first tasks of the evening was to chat with his opponent, Bob

Dole. You have to love politics—men who spent more than a year cutting each other down, calling each other everything except a son of God, ends up laughing and patting each other on the back, figuratively, after the race is done and the victor is called.

The president walked to the microphone shortly after 11 p.m. It was a while before he could get a word out. His 21-minute speech was interrupted more times than I could count with loud, thunderous, happy applause. After his speech, the Clintons and the Gores worked the last rope line of the last presidential campaign in the 20th century.

PART VI

AN AMERICAN PRESIDENCY

(1997–2000)

IV

1997 was an exceptionally good year for the Clinton presidency, but not one without hitches or political stumbles because we were human, and just as importantly, he was still fighting an uphill battle against a Republican-led Congress. Bill Clinton wouldn't be lucky enough in his entire eight years to experience an easy year.

In spite of the fact that much of the world had fallen in love with this American president, many of his own citizens and many in his own party would never claim the Hope, Arkansas, native as "one of us." He was, even after his re-election, still viewed as an outsider who slipped into the White House through the side door. Many die-hard conservatives continued to claim his lack of lineage and his too liberal social views as too dangerous for someone sitting in the Oval Office.

Bill Clinton, though, had proved his resiliency. He was back on his feet, had backed down House Speaker Newt Gingrich and the Republicans' "Contract with America." He'd kept many, if not all, of his promises made to the American people—to create a more economically sound country, to improve life in every sector of the country, to nurture global economics, and to get rid of waste in government, including an embarrassing federal deficit.

He had proved himself to be an astute politician and a strong leader. After a bumpy first term that included trying to learn how to be president and how to figure out who he should trust to help him become a better president, he'd done what he'd always done—learned from some dangerous mistakes. Unlike many other presidents, he hadn't simply accepted those mistakes.

Wisely, but with some hesitation, President Clinton replaced people and moved them around. Like a winning chess game, he was, by 1997, satisfied with the men and women who made up his close circle, his Cabinet and his advisers. These were the people who would help him get his agenda through. Also, by 1997, his opponents and enemies knew they weren't dealing with just a green Southern boy who was awfully nice and would do anything to be loved.

From the time I arrived in Washington until I left in 2001, I would always get the question: What is President Clinton really like? I never painted myself as one of his best friends or part of his close circle. Yes, I had known him for many years, had observed him during his long and successful leadership in Arkansas . . . and, yes, Arkansas was small enough that someone like me could meet a governor and from time to time chat with him.

Somehow, I overlooked the fact that even with his frequent public appearances, town hall meetings, speeches and campaign stops, most Americans had never seen this president, certainly not had a conversation with him.

Yet, when I was asked this rhetorical question, I immediately assumed they were asking for more than I was able to share with them. Likely, I wasn't being fair. Those of us who worked for him, became comfortable seeing him during the week, running into him in the hallway or walking from the residence to the West Wing.

How easily we forgot that to most of the world he was the president of the United States—an icon, an unreachable figure. To those of us who worked for him, he was human, reachable and still the president of the United States.

Sometimes, I'd simply say, "Oh, he's a really great guy," or "I love working for him. He's just as smart, as brilliant as you've heard . . . but he's also funny and really down to earth." Most times, I could see their eyes glaze over. That wasn't exactly what they wanted to hear. They wanted to hear what he was really like . . . who he was as a person.

People outside the White House and those inside and outside the Beltway wanted a bird's-eye view from someone who was in a position to have a bird's-eye view. They didn't want to hear the answers they could just as easily retrieve from the Internet or from watching a news conference or by paying $10 to watch some movie based on his presidency. Sitting in the seat appointed me as personal diarist to this president, who was this man whose life I observed so closely every working day for more than five years?

So in time, I began saying more, something more meaningful, and sharing anecdotes of what I'd seen or what he'd said. I was sure his years in Arkansas helped tell the story more than his years in Washington. I was sure that the presidency demanded that he show another side of the Bill Clinton we knew, not always the side we treasured most.

Yet, he was still the man from Hope. He was still the public servant that we knew and loved. But, yes, becoming president had demanded he add a layer to all that. It was called survival. I didn't know politics, but I knew a little about human nature. He had to protect himself, and he had to fight, probably more than most men who had worked so hard to sit in that seat.

He was a personality much too large for me to glibly explain. With my limited knowledge about psychology, I knew he must be so complex that even he didn't realize all the things that made him who he was.

─────

1998 promised to be more of the same for the Clinton presidency—moving forward, keeping his promises to America. No lame duck status for Bill Clinton; there was a great deal he wanted to do for America, still. We were all feeling redeemed, as we celebrated and welcomed in the New Year. He had been battered about so much during his first term, we were certain that good things awaited us these next three years.

Nothing would have convinced us that the last four years had actually been the good years, compared to what lay ahead. Nothing convinces us just how good we've really got it more than when something out of the clear blue sky happens to topple that illusion or reality.

The story of the Lewinsky sex scandal broke in January 1998 and changed the tenor of President Clinton's second term. What might the Clinton presidency have looked like in 1998 from those on the outside looking in? Would I remember that time the same way had I and other White House aides not been as intimately involved in Kenneth Starr's legal scuffle?

Wisdom often comes with a price so high that you wonder if it wouldn't be better to remain ignorant or blind. It was during those first months of 1998 that I saw clearly what Nancy Hernreich had said without saying:

Though my role as presidential diarist was important to this president, my role must never become a problem for the president.

In 1998, in the midst of all the anti-Clinton fervor, both my role and my diary were suddenly a problem. My naïve ambition to do the best job possible in chronicling the days of the Clinton presidency turned out to be red bait for those looking for red bait. There were questions about what I'd written, when I'd written it, about whom I'd written.

In my eyes, of course, there was only a desire to do my job. Political naiveté is no excuse, I now know. Was I horrified, dismayed that someone would find something wrong or even punishable that I'd done? You bet. I wasn't alone in this fear and dismay. I was just one of many White House aides subpoenaed for the infamous Kenneth Starr investigation. I had one interview inside the White House and another at the district courthouse. I wouldn't have dreamed, in a million years, my White House experience would be so all encompassing.

What was it like? How many times have I been asked that question? How many times have I tried to smile, to dodge or ignore this question? Of course, it was hell. It was one of the most horrible episodes in my 43 years—made worse by the knowledge that our nightmare was a reason for celebration for others. The vision of witless fish inside a humongous fishbowl, as they're being not only taunted, but shot at is a fitting description of what we all were feeling.

And, as this was happening in public view, we were all going through our own personal emotional turmoil. While I can only speak, categorically, for myself, there is little question in my mind and heart that others were feeling much the same.

That ominous cloud of disappointment, disillusion and fear fell so quickly, so silently over the White House and everyone inside. We had no idea what to do with these emotions, where to tuck them away as we went about our lives, our work.

How do you, on a dime, stop loving what you do each day? Stop holding the president you adulate ... in adulation? How do you reconcile not having that same excitement about getting up each morning and doing what you believe you were meant to do?

The silence was heavy and painful. We all imagined what the other was thinking, but no one was brave enough to say. We were angry and sad. The grief mixed with bitterness was sickening—a dangerous cocktail. So much so, that I found myself angry when some innocent, caring person asked simply, "How is the president coping ... how are you all taking all of this?"

In my own confused state, I saw this as a voyeur's question, and I refused to answer for the longest. It was a time most of us tried to block out, forget ... mask. In the president's own words, we "continued to do the work of the American people." It was not an easy task for those of us without the natural ability to compartmentalize their lives the way Bill Clinton could. A master at so many things, this trait would serve him well in 1998 and the rest of his presidency.

To say President Clinton received letters from his loyal followers and dejected friends during that dark period of his presidency would be a gross understatement. He received troughs full of long, cathartic ramblings by religious fanatics, testimonials for leaders who'd been there, sermons from the religious zealots and recriminations from rabid others who knew this would happen with a Democrat in the Oval Office.

There were also thousands of kind letters expressing love and continued confidence in the president. As only Bill Clinton can, he took them all seriously. Thus, we made sure he received them on a regular basis. He was being advised by laymen to publicly repent, step down, or face the music of letting Congress decide his future.

Most who followed President Clinton's speeches during the eight years of his presidency rated his speech—some called it a sermon—to the Convocation of the Church of God in Christ in Memphis, Tennessee, as one of his greatest. It was to many of the same leaders of this black religious group, plus others, that he was speaking. Many still believe that it is before these such audiences—black or white—that Bill Clinton most easily speaks from his heart.

If that is so, it makes sense that it was to this audience—this time inside the White House in the beautiful setting of the East Room—that President Clinton offered his first public repentance for an error the world had learned about over network television.

His audience that day was mostly made up of black religious leaders he knew quite well. This was the same Bill Clinton who had kept up with their families, called their names out loud before, during or after speeches. Shared "Amens" during their sermons and offered religious words of his own.

This was the same Bill Clinton who had imbued hope in them and their families and their communities during the decades when hope was in scarce supply. By the time he spoke to this group in the East Room on September 11, 1998, the morality storm that had engulfed him in January was fizzling down to little more than a dust storm. This audience of ministers and bishops and clergymen and women were friends, had been friends throughout his political career. This was his first public mention, first repentance for the sin. It wouldn't be his last.

Bill Clinton had always been able to depend on these men and women's friendships and support; and as friends, he asked for not only their forgiveness, but also their prayers. It was a heartfelt, but unusually short speech, for an unusually important subject. It was one of the few speeches, in most of these leaders' memories that Bill Clinton had prepared beforehand, including this one paragraph:

" . . . I have been on quite a journey these last weeks to get to the end of this, to the rock bottom truth of where I am and where we all are . . . I don't think there is a fancy way of saying I have sinned."

Those of us inside the White House would have to find other ways to purge the emotional turmoil, to eradicate the distorted mirror image of a small-town circus. For this moment in history, the mess surrounding the Clinton presidency mocked the many dreams and hopes we knew he had for America and its people.

In December 1998, just as I was starting to sleep through the night and get up most mornings and pretend the worst had come and gone, I was plopped right smack in the middle of the storm. Nancy's concern that the media might misconstrue my role at the White House was well grounded.

She had been wise in her tentativeness. Some members of the media wondered if my role included recording the president's thoughts and personal views of events. Some questioned whether I was filing away damnable documents that might be "smoking guns" in the Lewinsky affair.

In truth, I was merely a fly on the wall, charged only with documenting a day in the presidency from my own accounts, my personal observations and the use of White House documents I was able to review.

Nevertheless, I became a duel target of both the grand jury and the national media. When President Clinton told the grand jury on March 16, 1998, that Janis Kearney kept a diary of what went on in his day, it gave them a lead they hadn't had before. I became a small fish of interest in this sea of water.

For the next months, my life would be more and less than I'd ever imagined. My computer entries became important in this case. I became quite familiar with the president's White House counsel. For weeks, I traveled back and forth between my cubicle and the third floor where Cheryl Mills, Charles Ruff—and later Greg Craig, Lannie Davis, Lannie Breuer and the rest of the White House "dream team" resided.

If it hadn't been such a nightmare, I might have felt privileged to have Lannie Davis prepping me for the media questions—going over questions I was sure to get from the White House and other media across the country. Lannie Davis was the spokesman for the case, and I felt 100 percent more secure in that knowledge. He began by sharing with me a list of questions the media wanted answers to, including:

1. Who is Janis Kearney and what does she do?
2. What are her exact duties?
3. How long has she been at the White House?
4. To whom does she report?
5. How long has she been putting information into these summaries?
6. How did she obtain the information she puts into the summaries?
7. How often did she attend meetings? What kind of meetings would she attend?
8. Would she travel with the president?
9. Would she take notes? If so, where are the notes? Have they been turned over separately? If not, why not?
10. Would she ever record (video or audio) meetings or events?
11. Does she print out the summaries on a regular basis? Has she ever printed them out?
12. Did anybody except her have access to her computer? If so, did anybody review it on a regular basis? If so, when and why?
13. What information is encompassed in the summaries?
14. How does it differ from the diarist's index?
15. Do her summaries exist in printed form?

16. Does Ms. Kearney still create these daily summaries?
17. Has Ms. Kearney altered her activities in any way since the Counsel's office determined that some of her entries must be provided to the Congress and the Justice Department?
18. Why were the summaries created?
19. Whose idea was it?
20. Who was involved in the decision to create the summaries? Was the president or first lady?
21. Did the president know that Ms. Kearney was keeping these summaries? Did the vice president? Did the first lady? Did Mrs. Gore?
22. Prior to the production of these materials, who knew that Ms. Kearney creates these summaries?
23. Did the Counsel's office send a directive to Ms. Kearney or to the office of Oval Office Operations? If so, when? What directives?
24. When did the Counsel's office first learn of the computerized summaries?

My hometown newspaper, the Arkansas Democrat Gazette, ran a number of stories highlighting their hometown girl's White House troubles. On December 10, 1998, an Arkansas reporter's Associated Press submission entitled "White House Diary Shows Pressure and Cynicism" noted the senior staff meeting exchange I'd sat in on and cited in my daily diary.

The reporter wrote:

... The remarkable exchange, never meant to be public, is in notes belatedly turned over to congressional investigators—an informal diary that provides

> *a rare glimpse at the pressure-packed and sometimes cynical world of White House politics.*
>
> *The 200 pages of notes were written by presidential records manager Janis Kearney, a member of a long-respected Arkansas family with deep political ties to President Clinton. Her husband, Bob Nash, is White House personnel director. Administration officials said she began compiling the notes in 1995 as an informal supplement to the president's archives . . .*
>
> *Angry Republican investigators received the notes Monday night . . . in lean, undecorated language, Kearney details the president's schedule, summarizes news items and records private staff meetings. And she reveals a staff hardened by controversy and campaign pressure.*

The very next day, an *Arkansas Democrat Gazette* story, entitled "Clinton Notes Land Arkansan in Funding Fray," stated,

> *Former Arkansas journalist Janis Kearney chronicles President Clinton's daily activities for the White House archives, but her record keeping could make her a historical footnote in the campaign finance case.*

And, then there was the *Washington Times* column on December 11, 1998, entitled, "Dribs and Drabs of Documents," which said:

> *Monday night, after the evening news broadcasts had aired, the White House revealed that late last month it had discovered hundreds of pages of notes taken by a presidential aide responsible for recording the actions of the president . . .*

None of the lessons learned during my 40-plus-year journey prepared me for the 1998 event that the media dubbed the *Lewinsky Scandal*. It would have taken a lot more lessons and a lot more wisdom to prepare me for what came after the story hit the airways and Monica Lewinsky became a household name.

If a dollar had been miraculously deposited into my meager bank account each time I was asked to describe what the White House was like during that time, I would have been a much wealthier woman. Fortunately, I was never asked that question by close friends, family or people who held sincere admiration for the president or his White House. Yet, there have been plenty of people dying to know what it was like . . . or maybe just what I would say it was like.

I was never certain how to describe my emotions during that time. What was both comforting and troubling was that there were so many of us dealing with those indescribable emotions. It was not a feel-good time for those of us working for the Clinton administration. Yet, walking outside that complex each day gave us a different, clearer view of that presidency. We saw that this scandal threatened to allow his opponents to throw out the president with the bathwater.

Many of us, if not most of us, felt that our ideals, our political philosophies, the policies our president sought to put in place were really what was being attacked, placed under siege by the media and the Clintons' political enemies.

Even the American people, the general public—certainly smarter than most politicians—were drawn into this ugly drama for a time. And, for a time, it was too much for any of us to be hopeful it would end anytime soon.

Miraculously, after the first few weeks of intense scrutiny, we slowly began to wake from the horror of January and resume our jobs with as much hope for things to return to normal as we could muster. In spite of the raunchiness of the news reports, America was, in fact, in the midst of the best of times in decades. No matter what the outcome of the legal and political war, the Clinton era had changed much in America, much for everyday Americans.

Most promises had been kept, and it was clear that plans were on the table to make even more substantive changes for the American people. Many Americans—not all, certainly—were prospering beyond their wildest dreams. People I knew personally had choices in where they worked . . . if and where their children would attend college . . . even where they chose to live.

People with money were getting richer, and others who had enough to invest profited from those investments. Here, for the first time in American history, women, children, the ailing, the developmentally disabled—a larger cross-section of Americans—were reaping the benefits of a growing economy and good government policies. Americans felt safer, more confident, and more hopeful than they had in decades. And countries beyond our borders saw us as bigger and better . . . because we were.

Because we couldn't talk about this white elephant with each other, I thought about it a great deal—during and after work. Whether it was in spite of our painful humiliation or because of it, America would have to grow up when it came to our leaders. No one wants to hear there is no Santa Claus or that the stork doesn't actually deposit babies . . . but in the end the truth is worth the momentary hurt.

America needed to look at our presidents as great people who are still human and to vote for them based on what they could do for our country and its people, not what did or didn't happen in their most intimate lives. While the American presidency is about great men and great leadership, it has also been about maintaining an unrealistic myth.

There was never a perfect president. Neither was there ever a president elected because he willingly bared his flaws along with his strengths to the American people. None of us are graded on perfection in any other job.

Even though George Washington's presidency was a statement that America wanted to move away from monarchy, that we were seeking a more Democratic leadership than the kings and queens of England, there was still the innate need for the masses to believe their president, their leader, was something closer to a king than a common man.

Two hundred years later we have tried maintaining that myth. Thus, our media and political saboteurs can come very close to destroying a great president by saying he is merely a man. In truth, each of the men elected to the presidency were mere men. Some, in fact, were our greatest leaders, though they may have been considered the simplest of men.

Every president—maybe not every one—beginning with George Washington has had some innate or learned gift which the average American lacked.

The greatest of them was endowed with just the right mixture of leadership and humanity needed for that specific time in history. Who but George Washington could have better represented the new nation called America? A man of high military rank and an aura of humility and sound judgment was exactly what the people needed in 1789.

Franklin Roosevelt, easily one of America's top five greatest presidents, hid his useless limbs because he wisely feared that America couldn't accept a president with such blatant imperfections. Thus, he sought to offer America the illusion of greatness—as if his legs held his heart and brain. He was great, but he was also very, very lucky . . . and very, very human.

And then there was John Kennedy, a scared and unsure president who stole the hearts of all Americans with his youth, wit, style and lineage, while his wife created her own cultural revolution.

Even Ronald Reagan met America's needs for that time in history. Sometimes we need a little make-believe to get us through our harsh realities.

Who of these men or any of our American presidents could have withstood the scrutiny, the glare of the floodlights as William Jefferson Clinton? Who, in fact, would have remained committed to serving the American people in spite of those floodlights?

I'm still not absolutely sure what the questioners who are so adamant to know "what was it like," really want to hear. I know the time of which they speak—the dark era that is no more an indictment on the Clinton presidency than on the place to which partisan politics had sank.

Gratefully, I know far too little to whet their appetites for anything salacious. But beyond that, if the expectation is that I might say that as an American, my president let me down or that I lost all respect and reverence for him or the office, neither would be farther from the truth.

The truth is, the five years of my role in the Clinton presidency served to convert me from a sideline politician to one who now preaches the importance of politics in our lives . . . every facet of our lives.

I hold no illusions about the purity or goodness of man. God made us in his image. That certainly means his physical image, not the makeup of our hearts and souls. God knows we aren't perfect and loves us anyway. Why would any of us believe a man is perfect or more set in God's image because he sits in the Oval Office?

Our 42nd president played a huge role in convincing me that a president can do unbelievable good if he or she chooses to use their time in the White House to do so. I saw that in Bill Clinton's leadership, in his policies, in his everyday decisions, and in his presidency. I also witnessed it in his doggedness to include all Americans in the American dream.

How many times have we, who worked in the Clinton administration, been tagged blind loyalists? Nothing could be farther from the truth . . . a loyalist, most definitely, but hardly blind. I'm my father's daughter. I am too much of a realist to be a blind loyalist. I see all people, even the ones I admire the most, as a combination of good and not so good.

Some of our greatest leaders have led despicable personal lives. Yet, their greatness was in helping change the country and the world for the better. Their goodness was that they chose to use God's gifts to improve the lives of others, in spite of their personal shortcomings.

Our 42nd president was, even after the storm, that man from Hope, Arkansas, who had an idealist desire to change America from what it was to what it could be. He was a brilliant, charismatic leader whose human flaws were placed under a microscope and looked bigger than they were and overshadowed so much of the good he did.

What would men do without the silver linings, the rainbows, and the sunshine after the rain? If we can just wait out the storm, there is almost always a brighter day ahead. I know from experience, from the many childhood nights I went to bed hungry and woke up the next morning to realize that not only had the hunger disappeared, but in its place was a clearer mind and a new way of looking at life.

One byproduct of the cloud that settled for a time over 1600 Pennsylvania Avenue was Bob and I rediscovering normalcy in our own lives. We realized that there was life and even some joy that could be had outside that fishbowl called the White House. We wanted and needed those small snippets of normalcy and happiness for our sanity and well-being.

We also realized that there were many of our colleagues learning this simple lesson, too. We'd see each other outside the White House gates and grin—no explanation needed—as if to say, "Yes, there is life outside the fishbowl."

It was during this time we became almost normal married people. Washington is the best place in the world to do the things that normal people do. Yet, most people who live there ignore that fact. Most who immigrate to D.C. aren't looking for the simple, everyday joys of life. Instead, they're seeking that aphrodisiac called power. They expect to find it, and many do, inside places like the White House, the halls of Congress, the swank lobbyists' offices or the large government departments.

Existing inside the Beltway is indeed an exciting place to be, and the ability to rub shoulders with those who make decisions gives most people a natural high. It is an intoxicating place, and few people will give much thought to something as mundane as a normal life until they're forced to, until they're faced with the humanity of those in power and the downside to it all.

Bob and I had talked since arriving in D.C. about getting to know the city and the many historical surrounding towns. How many of us had made that idle promise when we arrived in 1993.

Most of our friends admitted they'd never visited the historical museums like the museums of Women's History, African American History, Aviation, Photography, Arts, or even the place that would eventually house my and other White House employees' work documents—the National Archives. I'd developed a love for history from my father, and there was no better place to satisfy that love than Washington.

In spite of the rocky relationship the White House had with the media, I met a lot of good people who just happened to be reporters who were part of the White House media pool. These are the men and women whose second home is on the White House grounds, and they very often are the ones who travel with the president throughout his terms.

When you wonder how the president knows the names of certain reporters, it's because he sees some of them on a weekly basis and they ride Air Force One with him.

Because I rarely traveled on international trips with the president, I enjoyed reviewing the reporters' pool reports composed during their travels with the president. I wasn't surprised that the reports were so well written. These were reporters from major print and broadcast bureaus, after all.

I was surprised, though, to see just how in-depth they were in their reports. They picked up on so many small nuances and shared tidbits of information that added to the report. One of the more interesting reports was about the president's trip to St. Petersburg, Russia. The details of that visit took my breath away.

The reporter gave me a completely different view of Russia, an appreciation for its history and beauty. They described a conversation the president had with the curator in a St. Petersburg museum, and the curator's lengthy and thorough explanation of the history of the infamous city of St. Petersburg.

I also received handwritten notes from the president's personal aide Steve, Butt Boy as we called him, and later his replacements Kris and Doug. Their notes offered a few of their own observations about our president's travels around the world.

While our country is a mere toddler in comparison to ancient Europe, Asia and Africa, we have magnificent history and art right in front of our noses. Over the next year, Bob and I reclaimed some of our weekends—forcing ourselves to plan our workdays a little more efficiently to take advantage of our weekends. We even started taking weekend trips to surrounding sites like Mount Vernon, St. Michael's Island and Gettysburg, Pennsylvania. Even as far away as Philadelphia.

Though our jobs could be all consuming, I can only imagine how pretentious we must have sounded to friends and family, going on and on about having no time for ourselves, leaving the unspoken caveat that there was certainly no time for friends or family. We offered self-deprecating smiles when they sympathized with us. What we didn't say was that oftentimes that choice was largely ours to make.

The president really didn't demand that his aides work like he did. No critic ever called Bill Clinton a micromanager. In fact, he was a proponent of his aides spending time with their families. There was never any doubt that he wanted his work done, and done well, but like most smart managers, he left it to our own designs how we would get it done.

It was also up to us whether our work would take all of our weekends or just part of them. We didn't need to prove to anyone how committed we were to the president or his administration, we showed it through our work. So, weekends became at least partly ours.

There are moments within each experience that stand out and that make that experience more memorable because of that particular moment. There was such a moment during the Clinton presidency.

There was, in fact, a very long list of amazing events to take place during his eight years in office—Bill Clinton's visit to the eight countries in Africa; his apology for slavery at Senegal's Gorée Island; his acknowledgment and apology to the victims and survivors of the Tuskegee syphilis experiment; his posthumous Presidential Award to Captain Henry O. Flipper, the first black graduate of West Point who was wrongly accused of treason; and his close and enduring friendship with South African President Nelson Mandela.

There were the president's historical global initiatives, peace treaties, and summits for peace with world leaders. There was also his participation in helping to heal the wounds caused by the Oklahoma bombing, the 1963 Birmingham church bombings, the Arkansas and Colorado school killings, the threats of terrorist attacks. All of these would be a part of the Clinton legacy.

There was one event that would likely not be high on the president's list of legacies, but it served to paint a picture of the Bill Clinton I was in awe of as much as anything else he ever did.

We were already into the year 2000 and were joking that we already had one foot out the door of the White House. But President Clinton was still getting up each Saturday morning and walking over to the Oval Office to tape his live radio addresses. Buddy, his beautiful brown Labrador retriever, was his constant companion. And if he wasn't too rowdy, he could sit beside the president's desk as he taped his address.

A letter from Charlotte Fillmore's grandson arrived on Ben Johnson's desk in the spring of 2000, partly because Ben was the director of the president's One America Race Initiative office. The letter, in essence, stated that Mrs. Fillmore was celebrating her 100th birthday and that her one fervent wish was to visit the White House. But this time she didn't simply want to visit the White House, she wanted to enter through the front door.

We were all excited to have Mrs. Fillmore celebrate her 100th birthday at the White House, but were more than a little mystified by this request about coming through the front door. That is, until we learned the history between the White House and Mrs. Fillmore.

Charlotte Fillmore had visited the White House before . . . many times and many years earlier. She had, in fact, worked in the White House as a seamstress for Mrs. Mamie Eisenhower. Yet, in all of those years she served as seamstress to the first lady, Charlotte Fillmore had never walked into the White House through the main entrance. She had always been ushered through the servant's quarter—something like the "back door," she'd said.

President Clinton learned about Charlotte Fillmore's letter and was more than a little interested in meeting the seamstress of Mrs. Eisenhower. No doubt, the politician in him saw this as another opportunity to play up his One America Race Initiative, as well. This grandchild of slaves, who had worked for a first lady, was a wonderful poster child for that message.

The organizers of this event chose the president's Saturday morning radio address as a perfect time to invite Charlotte Fillmore into the White House. Like most

Saturday mornings before the radio addresses, President Clinton was able to sleep later than on weekdays, so he was in a chipper mood.

The plan was for the president to walk out to the front door, greet Charlotte and escort her through the front door of the White House. No one, however, had mentioned that the century-old Charlotte Fillmore was wheelchair-bound.

The president didn't miss a beat. He walked through the reception area that was already crowded with guests for the morning's radio address, offered a chipper good morning to the group, then walked directly through the door to greet the guest of honor.

There sat a beaming Charlotte Fillmore, as if she'd waited her whole life for this moment. President Clinton smiled as if he had, too. After greeting the beautifully coiffed woman, he placed one Happy Birthday kiss on her cheek and said a loud "Welcome to the White House" that still held a bit of Southern drawl.

He shook hands with the nephew who was the impetus of this special day and thanked him for letting Ben Johnson know about Mrs. Fillmore's birthday wish. Then, the president took possession of the elderly woman's chair, as if he'd pushed wheelchairs for a living at some point in his life. In they went through the front door of the White House as television cameras rolled and still photographers snapped pictures all around them.

The crowd quickly formed an aisle as they looked on at this tall, stately woman being chauffeured by the president of the United States. Charlotte Fillmore wore the most beautiful smile of happiness during that entire 45-second walk to the Oval Office.

Once there, the president allowed one of his aides to arrange her chair beside the sofa. As he prepped for the address, she became the center of attention. There was no question, she was used to and loved attention. There was no indication that this was her first visit to the Oval Office. She chatted graciously with the White House aides, thanking them for their warm birthday wishes.

Charlotte Fillmore's smile didn't leave her face once during the hour or so she sat in the Oval Office. She listened attentively as the president delivered his radio address, and she even blushed when he wished her a Happy Birthday on the air.

After the address, as the president greeted his long line of visitors, it was clear that Charlotte had her own entourage of fans. Without a trace of shyness, she shared stories about her years as Mamie Eisenhower's seamstress and her later years as a schoolteacher in the D.C. area. It was a day Charlotte Fillmore wouldn't soon forget.

President Clinton had spent less than an hour in the company of Charlotte Fillmore, but that hour meant more to the centenarian than anything any of us could have imagined.

Charlotte Fillmore passed away the next year, but President Clinton, his gracious invitation and personally chauffeuring her into the White House, must have been some of the memories that traveled with her through that final door.

By August 2000, our White House days seemed to be passing twice as quickly as they had even a year earlier. Much of the interoffice conversations now were about what came next in our lives. A growing number of aides chose the year 2000 as their "jumping off" period—hoping to parlay their experiences and time in the White House into something lucrative in the real world.

Bob and I hadn't talked seriously about leaving before January 20, 2001. But we were beginning to talk more about the next chapter in our lives. The unspoken thought on the minds of many White House aides was: "How do we top eight years with the president?" I had pretty much decided the last half of my life would be devoted to writing and possibly some teaching. Bob, on the other hand, didn't seem to want to think too much about the next chapter.

My brother, Jude, who had worked for Ron Brown at the Department of Commerce, had left that job two years earlier to take a partnership with the international law firm, LeBoef Lamb. Most of his tenure there, so far, had been in the international realm, and he'd done most of his work in South Africa. In 2000, he was invited by the firm to open and manage a new office in Johannesburg.

We were all very excited about this move for Jude and Lorraine. Their two children—Kathryn, 8, and Jude Jr., 12, were both excited, too, except when they remembered they were leaving their schools, their grandparents, their best friends, and everything they had ever known.

In the midst of all of this excitement, nothing would have prepared me for the August night that completely ruined the wonderful farewell celebration Bob and I had enjoyed as we said our final goodbyes to Jude and his family before their imminent departure to South Africa.

I hadn't thought of Rodney King and his terrible police brutality tragedy for years. The thought of horrible police harassments and beatings just isn't something most of us keep on our minds, unless we witness it on a news report or read about it in our newspapers.

Other than that, it's the kind of thing you can't afford to think about constantly if you want to hold onto your sanity. Besides, there just wasn't a lot about Rodney King I identified with—except the obvious, we were both African Americans. The similarities pretty much ended there.

At least they had until August 2000. Suddenly, our similarities became more than just the color of our skin. No, Bob and I were not beaten senseless by Los Angeles cops, nor did we experience even a percentage of what Rodney King did in brutality or harassment.

Yet, more than ever before, on that August night in Montgomery County, Maryland, we finally understood some of what he must have been feeling on his fateful night. I imagined the humiliation and rage that must have coursed through Rodney King's veins during the atrocious experience of unprovoked violence at the hands of L.A. police.

Ironically, the night had been a happy celebration dinner at Jude and Lorraine's home. We spent the evening with the two of them, their two children, and Lorraine's family from Pittsburgh and Virginia. It was a night of cheer, celebration, love and happiness. Bob and I were happy and proud of Jude's opportunity for this new experience, and of Lorraine's bravery in sharing this new adventure.

Jude deserved this. A Harvard economics graduate and Stanford lawyer, he was one of my younger and quite brilliant brothers, who had always made the family proud. He'd worked hard during his time with Secretary Brown, as an assistant secretary for Global Initiatives and was likely still working just as hard.

Before coming to the Department of Commerce, Jude had worked for the Jones Day firm, headquartered in New York. It hadn't been long after Secretary Brown's death that Jude had left the Department to take a partnership with LeBeof Lamb.

In Johannesburg, he would open and take on the managing directorship of the company's first firm in South Africa. Lorraine and the kids would follow after the end of the school year.

The evening had been casual and fun with lots of laughter and some tears. Bob and I, though, still had to get up for our early morning meetings at the White House. So we said goodbye earlier than we really wanted to.

After Bob's toast, we exchanged more hugs and said our good nights. Bob and I joked that Jude and Lorraine lived too far out in Montgomery County for friends to visit.

"We're like everybody else, trying to get away from black folks ... " Jude joked, as always getting the last word.

It was the kind of evening that left a smile on your face all during your ride back home. Or one you'd end up calling a friend or sibling and talking about to keep the good feeling going a while longer. In spite of Bob's half joking complaint, the return traffic wasn't bad during the drive between Montgomery County and our home in northwest D.C. We discussed Jude's job, the excitement of working in South Africa and even some about what our futures might look like.

We both heard the police sirens, and I turned to see the bright lights of fast approaching cars. I suggested to Bob that he slow down to let them past.

"I wonder what's going on up farther," I said, as Bob and I both peered through the windshield to see if there was an accident or something.

But as we looked in our rear view mirror, we both noticed the twirling lights of one police car, and then more, coming to a halt behind us. Another, with glaring lights, rushed quickly in front of us, then swerved to block our car.

"Stop! Turn off your engine and step out of the car with your hands up! NOW!" It was the beginning of a horrible nightmare. It was no more real for me than those nightmares I use to have while growing up on Varner Road—the ones Mama called "witches riding your dreams" that we couldn't wake up from no matter how hard we tried.

But, unlike that night, those bad dreams usually concerned floods, fires, being lost or separated from my parents, being chased by murderers—all the bad things children imagine can happen in their lives.

Bob and I looked quickly at each other with perplexed looks on our faces. Ironically, neither of us spoke. We were scared speechless. This was a new experience, and we had no idea what the outcome might be. Except, I was remembering Rodney King by then . . . and all the other news reports I'd watched, then forgotten.

A policeman appeared quickly at each of our doors. We let our windows down. Bob was told to get out first, then me. Our hands were already up. What a strange feeling. I'd seen this on television. I hadn't seen many women in this predicament, but I knew I was far from the first.

"Raise your hands up where we can see them!" I thought of my son and my nephews and my brothers and Bob's son and all the young men who might very well have experienced such a horrible event in their lives. It was an event that would always stay with me, always haunt me, always make it more difficult for me to see good policemen—as many are—with the kind of pride and sense of security that I should.

As they held their guns directed at us, at our heads to be exact, we were commanded to back up, rather than walk forward, to the back of our car, a recently purchased dark blue 1997 Q24 Mitsubishi sports utility vehicle.

There were no faces, just policemen's uniforms, badges, and guns. I wouldn't be able, ever, to say exactly how many there were. There were more than five large rifles pointed at our heads, possibly closer to 10. They were all white and all men, except for one woman. She would speak, later.

They immediately turned us around, and as Bob tried to ask them what the problem was, they warned him to keep quiet. As they pulled our arms behind us and began to handcuff us, one policeman, maybe the leader, radioed into someone describing the SUV and us. Finally, he asked if we had any identification. Bob told them he had a driver's license and a business card in his pocket. The officer took the information from his pocket, went to his car and sat there talking to someone on his radio.

He returned in what seemed like hours. "These aren't the ones . . . we can let them go." They unlocked our handcuffs. No other words were spoken by any of the policemen, including the leader. The woman whispered, "We're sorry about this . . ."

I didn't respond or look at her. By then, I was trembling with rage and fear. Bob hugged me for just a moment before leading me to the passenger side of the car. Bob knows me, he was still afraid, shaken; but I was angry, enraged, and he knew it. His fear was as much about how I would react, as how the policemen would.

That was a major difference in my husband and me. I could never exhibit his kind of restraint, the kind that would keep him safe, when my anger could very easily have gotten us shot—with cause. Bob's thoughts jumped forward to what would happen next. Mine were still in the present in the middle of feeling a sense of rage and injustice. Had it not been for Bob's methodical thinking, I likely would have gotten us both shot, maybe killed, or at least handcuffed and hauled off to jail that night.

Bob and I looked at each other for a minute as we sat in the car. We were both too shaken to voice what we were feeling or thinking. I was crying nonstop by then, and Bob's face had set in a hard anger that I recognized.

When we finally arrived home, Bob went directly to his office and got on the phone. He made calls to the Sheriff's Department and then to the Attorney General's office, though he must have known no one would be there at midnight.

He left a message that would be shared with many people in the administration and the White House by the next day. Bob asked for Montgomery County Police

Chief Charles Moose and was told that Moose was not available.

At Bob's request, Moose's office finally faxed the description of the two people they had been looking for that night. It was a young, black man in his 20s, light complexion and bald. Bob is dark-complexioned, was then in his late 40s, and had a full head of hair. The young man had a girlfriend with him, likely in her 20s, as well. I certainly didn't fit that description.

Bob kept up the calls until early morning and even the next day. He received several calls from the Attorney General's office, but never a call and certainly not an apology from Chief Moose, who happened to be an African American—like Bob and Rodney King and me. I wondered if he might have a young son.

What I immediately began to tell myself after the police stop, after our humiliation of being forced from our car with more shotguns leveled at us than I'd ever seen in my lifetime, is that it could have been worse. My mind immediately went to Rodney King, then later to other young men who experienced the same terror, the same humiliation, and for some, the same horrifying beatings as Rodney King or worse.

But it's still hard to settle for "it could have been worse," when it was so obviously wrong—something that should have never happened and not the way it happened. I can imagine slaves telling their children who feel the scars on their backs, "it could have been worse, baby."

I also imagine the women, who are humiliated by the attorneys and the public a second time after they have been brutally raped, trying to convince themselves:

"But it could have been worse ... at least he didn't kill me." Yes, our situation could have been worse. But why in 2000 should it have happened in the first place?

More than anything that had happened to me in my earlier life, I now understood how one seemingly small incident might change one's life forever. As Bob and I finally rode home in too much shock to even nurture each other's pain, I imagined there had been thousands of young men and women who experienced this very thing. And because we, the baby boomers want to believe it, we teach our children that in the end justice always prevails ... that if they keep a level head, everything will turn out fine.

The truth is, for too many Americans, justice does not prevail in the end. Injustice and unequal justice still runs rampant in our judicial systems. And believing that it could have been worse doesn't address the emotional scars left on a young or old or middle-age person's psyche after experiencing an incident like ours.

It is incidents such as this that helps fuel the rage we pretend not to understand in so many young men we interact with each day. Their belief in justice slowly but surely changes into disillusion, and when an incident like ours comes along, that disillusion turns to outrage and finally to rage. Horrible things happen in the name of, and because of, rage.

Gratefully, we were older, more mature and had enough outlets to suffuse most of the rage. Most of it. It would be an untruth to say that there is no remnant of rage still inside me from that incident. I don't discuss that night with anyone, not even Bob. I can't ... it's still too painful.

It was my father who taught me that freedom should also mean justice. It was he who taught me that injustice is a sin just as stealing or killing. I abhor injustice in any form. And, sadly, I am convinced that if an incident such as ours could happen in 2000, we are yet a long, long way from creating that mythological "justice for all," and that enrages me.

Bob and I decided we wouldn't move forward with legal remedy because we both wanted to put the horrifying incident behind us. We didn't want the media attention that was already starting. There were phone calls from a number of news outlets interested in interviews.

We agreed . . . no media. We didn't, in truth, want to be the poster children for police profiling or to see this issue gain momentum only because we were part of the Clinton administration. That would be a slap in the face to all the thousands of young black men pulled over, strip searched, harassed, beaten, and even killed; who had nothing to do with the Clinton administration.

Putting an end to hate crimes; making race just a word, not a reason to discriminate; doing away with police profiling—all of these were initiatives that had been discussed and were important to our White House and administration. But that didn't change the fact that they were being actively practiced each and every day.

While we both believed that our administration was serious about changing America for the better, we also knew just how deep the root of evil grows. And we knew, all too well, just how slow that change would be.

PHOTOS

Something to Write Home About

A Photo Journey

Pictures are worth so much more than words. They dredge up memories of people and times in our lives like nothing else can. This photo collage chronicles 30 years of my life—from my last days on Varner Road to my last days at the Clinton White House. What an incredible journey!

I. Varner Road

1. Janis Faye Kearney's graduation photo, from Gould High School, 1971
2. Portraiture of Ethel Virginia Curry Kearney, circa 1945
3. Author between classes at the University of Arkansas, Fayetteville, with six-month-old D.K., 1974
4. Kearney patriarch James Kearney and Jeffery, during Kearney reunion, 1998
5. Author and family members pose at an early Kearney reunion, circa 1975. Standing: Janeva, John, Janis, Julius, Janetta and Jesse. Front: Jude (with nephew John-John) and Jo Ann (with nephew Brandon)
6. Another Kearney gathering, circa 1985

II. Daisy Bates and the State Press Years

7. Daisy Bates, author, and an unidentified artist, circa 1988

8. Governor Bill Clinton presents prestigious KARK-TV Citizenship Award to Daisy Bates, circa 1985.

9. Daisy Bates, author (standing, 2nd from left), and Bates Scholarship Committee review documents at scholarship selection meeting, 1989.

10. Author interviews Governor Bill Clinton about his presidential aspirations, 1990.

11. Daisy Bates and author converse during State Press anniversary celebration, 1993.

III. White House Years

My years inside the White House were amazing at so many levels. The one most memorable part of that time was the opportunity to watch presidential history in the making; to see men and women carry out the ideals of serving the American people one day after another. It was an awesome and a humbling experience that made me prouder to be an American than at any other time in my life. And, in the midst of all the work, there were light moments and even laughter. (Many of the White House photos used in this photo collage are courtesy of the William J. Clinton Library.)

12. Author and other Arkansans pose in front of the White House for Madame magazine article on Arkansans in the White House, June 1993. From left: Nancy Ward, Ashley Adams, Janis F. Kearney and Patti Cogdell.

13. Author serves cookies to the media at a post-election press conference in 1992.

14. Author and fellow White House Media Affairs staffers, Time magazine, 1993

15. Author, with husband, Bob Nash (right); fellow Arkansan Carol Willis (left); and General and Mrs. Colin Powell, November 1993

Personal Diarist to President Clinton

16. Author, with Deputy Chief of Staff Evelyn Lieberman and White House Secretary Betty Currie, on President Clinton's 21st Century rain ride through Middle America, 1996

17. Author and Betty Currie look on as President Clinton shows off his fishing hat, 1997.

18. Author, with President Clinton, 1998

19. A White House birthday celebration with fellow Oval Office aide, Kris Engskov, 1999

20. President Clinton enters the digital age as author and White House aides look on, 1999.

21. Author flanked by Nancy Hernreich, director, Oval Office Operations, and Betty Currie during annual White House Turkey Pardon, 1998

22. Author and former SBA Director Erskine Bowles, 1999

23. Author chats with First Lady Hillary Rodham Clinton during a White House event, 1999.

24. Author, Betty Currie and Deputy Media Affairs Director Beverly Barnes on a helicopter flight during President Clinton's historic Africa trip, 1998

25. Author with D.K. and daughter-in-law, Pamela, at Hugh Masekela event at the Kennedy Center, 2000

26. Author and Betty Currie greet Charlotte Fillmore—former seamstress to First Lady Mamie Eisenhower—during a White House radio address, 2000.

27. The Kearney family celebrates their annual reunion, at the White House, 1999.

28. Author enjoys a White House event with White House aide, the late Justin Coleman.

29. Author (standing, far right) travels home aboard Air Force One with President Clinton and fellow Arkansans: (from left) Bruce Lindsey, Rodney Slater, Bob Nash, unidentified, unidentified, Gloria Cabe, B.A. Rudolph, Carol Willis, Nancy Hernreich and Patsy Thomasson (seated next to President Clinton), 1998

30. Author and husband, Bob, on safari during President Clinton's trip to Africa, 1998

Who's Who at the President's House

One facet of living a dream during the Clinton years was the opportunity to not only meet celebrities, but also the chance to see firsthand that they are humans, first and foremost. The opportunity and the realization was an experience I never would have expected in my "real" world.

1. Author chats with basketball great Michael Jordan, 1997.
2. Author and tennis star Serena Williams, 1999
3. Author with music icon Billy Joel, 1998
4. Author and global humanitarian and musician, Bono, 1999
5. Author with Will Smith and wife, Jada Pinkett Smith, 1998

6. Whoopi and author at the White House, 2000
7. Author with reggae artist Wyclef, 2000
8. Author chats with civil rights icon Rosa Parks during a 21st Century train stop, 1996.
9. Author meets TV's "West Wing" president, Martin Sheen, 2000.
10. Author and Hollywood legendary actor Sidney Poitier, 1999

11. Author and blues great, B.B. King, 2000
12. Author with dramatic actress, Donzaleigh Abernathy, of Lifetime's "Any Day Now," and daughter of the late civil rights leader, Reverend Ralph Abernathy, 2000
13. Author with "Sound of Music" actress Julie Andrews, in the Oval Office, 2000
14. Author and pro tennis player, Andre Agassi, 2000
15. Author with TV's "West Wing" presidential aide, Dule Hill, and parents, 2000.

Goodbye to a Dream

The days leading up to January 20, 2001, were some of the most melancholy of my eight years of magic. I would have to say goodbye to friends, and colleagues who had become friends, and family who had been fellow celebrants during the good times and allies during the bad . . .

16. Author dons her "farewell" hat, with director of White House photography, Sharon Farmer.
17. Author shares laughs with longtime White House butler James Allen.
18. Author with White House military aides
19. Author says goodbye to White House mess staff.
20. The wisdom of eight years left in a note to the new president, January 20, 2001

EPILOGUE

The Journey

(January 20, 2001)

It is January 20, 2001, exactly eight years since the day I walked into the White House for the very first time. Those years have been a lifetime and more. Today, I am reintroduced to reality and find that the world and I have changed in that time, as well as every facet of my life and my family's life.

In my immediate family, I find the children are now adults, some beginning to start families of their own. Daddy is now on the brink of becoming a centenarian. God, what he has seen of this world! So few things remain today as they were on that cold morning of January 20, 1993, when I walked through the northwest gate, hardly daring to believe this was my new reality.

Someone said that every experience, each encounter in life, changes us a little. I am surely then changed from the person who nervously and timidly entered the White House that day. Yet, I recall more than nervous fear. I recall the boundless hope, the gratitude, the awe and a sense of expectation as I walked onto these hallowed grounds. As I walk away now, I pray I am leaving this place not just older, but wiser.

It is my last day at the White House. Even with all that took place during these eight years, it seems the years passed quickly. I tell myself there simply wasn't enough time to do all the things I promised. I don't want to think about the many backburner projects I pushed aside, promising myself, "I'll get to these, after January 20th."

I haven't been the best daughter or sister or friend since 1993. Few of us can claim we've been all we could have outside the walls of the White House. We found it amazingly easy to justify our shortcomings by the importance of our jobs and the place where we worked, going so far as telling ourselves we had to shut out much of our lives that didn't include this orbit of importance.

It didn't take long for me to understand why the divorce rate for politicians, including White House aides, is higher than the average rate. It makes sense that few married couples work in this environment. Someone has to keep his or her head in the real world. But it's not just the jobs. It's all that come with it, the power and excitement that come with the presidency, the existence inside his bubble.

That sense of being on the inside, knowing what will happen in the real world a minute or even a few seconds before it happens ... and certainly before the real world knows.

I find myself thinking of our lives in terms of childhood tales. Our return to normalcy begins at noon today—when the young George W. Bush takes over the presidency and the White House. It is the end of our Cinderella ball; and we, the poor stepsisters, are ushered back into a life of reality, old pumpkins and lost shoes in tow.

Bob and I discuss the next phase in our lives. I, along with nine other aides, will maintain one slippered foot inside the Clinton bubble for another six months, working in the president's transition office on 17th Street.

The Journey (January 20, 2001)

After that, I'll be treading on unslipped feet as well; and together Bob and I will ride off into reality . . . obscurity.

I am Dorothy in "The Wizard of Oz," telling myself that, while there is no place like home, it is not always so simple to go home again, after all. There is a comfort in knowing that Arkansas and Varner Road will always be there; and we know that day will come. But it will take a while, after eight years of living an impossible dream, to shake all the stardust off our shoulders. When we do, and we will, it will be past time.

These eight years have been so much more than I knew to expect or to even imagine. I witnessed more than I would have ever asked to see. I'd come through OK, but not as fast or as smoothly as I would have thought. Little did I know, it would take months before my feet would truly be on solid ground or that the adrenaline that kept me and others going inside those walls would remain for just a short time as we journeyed back into the real world.

The young White House aides down the hall and across the walk in the "Old Building" have been calling today, January 20, 2001, D-Day for the last month or so. It is the last day of the Clinton administration. It is the end to an eight-year dream, and the beginning of a new chapter for many of us.

The Clinton presidency has been many things, but boring isn't one of them, I think to myself as I enter the West Wing. The small office, which includes my tiny cubicle, has been home away from home for the last five years. This room of cubicles housed five presidential aides and an intern.

"Location, location, location" was what White House aides said mattered most, even as they joked about the crowded spot located just three doors down from the Oval Office. Of course, I had been clueless. I had always believed that space, not location, was the priority.

When Nancy Hernreich, the president's Oval Office director, showed me where I'd be stationed, I'd swallowed hard and reminded myself where I was. As I was being introduced to the roomful of young aides, all half my age, I was still turning over in my head that my new office was just a cubicle, separated from my colleagues by a single, gray cloth partition.

The young Texan who turned out to be the president's personal aide, half-whispered to me, "This is prime real estate. There are senior aides with huge offices in OEOB who would kill to get this close to the president."

It took me a while to grasp this D.C. logic, especially when the Old Executive Office Building was just a hop and a skip from where we sat and had spacious offices with real wood furniture and floor-to-ceiling windows. But, according to my new neighbor, most presidential aides would give up those beautiful offices in exchange for my tiny cubicle "in a New York minute!"

It didn't take long to realize just how far Little Rock, Arkansas, really is from the White House. I was in for an education, a roller-coaster ride with wonderful and sad and eye-opening memories to take away with me.

When I did have time to look up and take a deep breath, I realized that the life I had put on hold for years had gone on without me. It hadn't stopped because I wasn't there to be a part of it. My son had graduated from college, and I was now officially a middle-aged woman already experiencing some of the changes I'd only read about before moving here.

Maybe the most heart-wrenching experience was finding that time had finally caught up with my father, who had seemingly held on to youth for almost 90 years. We had all decided he would remain 50 for the rest of his days. But at 90, he was finally moving slower; and the light in his eyes was dimming just enough for those of us who knew him to notice.

Without making a big to-do about it, he'd given up his yearly bus and train tours of the country. His main goal was to visit his children, but he always returned with new friends. We couldn't help but feel proud of our aged father's independence. But we did worry a little more each time he climbed the steps of a bus or train.

I now understood what White House veterans said about the inevitable fear that life simply left you behind or the fear of finding or rediscovering one's niche out in the real world.

Like so many others, I had buried myself in the cocoon of the White House, using it as an excuse for ignoring what was going on outside its realm. Now I was on the brink of venturing back out into that reality, and it was a little frightening.

I stand in the middle of the room, scanning the small space that had been mine for more than five years. How fleeting now, that seat at the center of power.

At 10:02 a.m., I sit alone at the hardwood desk that would remain mine for another hour and 58 minutes. The big-faced clock's loud ticking is something I'd hardly noticed before. At noon, people like me will become former White House aides.

I collect the artifacts, pictures, mementos, speeches and letters from my desk and wall. My memory wall comes down, joining the heap of other keepsakes in a cardboard box. Days, weeks ago, colleagues had stopped by my cubicle and stooped to see what new photos I had taped to my wall.

I would offer my same excuse: I was born in the middle of a cotton field in southeast Arkansas, and the only celebrity we knew at the time was the infamous "Rag Man" who traveled the rural roads selling, from a backpack, all kinds of rags he'd collected.

I'd learned during my years here that the *beautiful people*, the celebrities, the big names and faces we held in such esteem were all simply people. Most were amazingly nice. Almost everyone I'd met was more enthralled with meeting the president of the United States than I was enthralled with meeting them.

I smile back at the smiling faces of Whoopi Goldberg, Robert De Niro, Bono, Julie Andrews, Venus and Serena Williams, Will and Jada Pinkett Smith, Andre Agassi, Sammy Sosa, and cast members from television shows such as "ER" and "The West Wing."

One day, I'll share these photos with my grandkids and maybe even to other geriatric patients in some old folks home where I'd sit during my remaining years reminiscing about the past. Although I am standing with

The Journey (January 20, 2001)

the *beautiful people* in the photos, we are all small stars in a surreal orbit with one blazing star at its core.

"Hey, I'm here to swipe your computer . . . "

I look up to see who has roused me from my daydreams. There stands a young, dark man with hair like Elvis Presley falling into his left eye. He is here to erase data from my computer, leaving my hard drive clean—a clean slate for the next aide who sits here.

"I need a minute. Can you work on another computer while I finish up?"

He scowls, doesn't answer, but saunters to another desk. I return to the accumulating pile on my desk, unhappy that I won't be able to complete this ceremony in solitude.

The temperature is near freezing today. I imagine there is something magical about January 20th that won't allow the temperature to move above 40 degrees. Unlike eight years ago, there is no sunshine today. The sky is cast in an ugly gray.

It is not a beautiful day to say goodbye to an old life. A light mist is falling, and it threatens to snow. Dampness permeates the city and now seeps into this room. Even as the sun peeks briefly through the overcast sky, the heaviness of the morning doesn't lighten. On second thought, it is a perfect day to say goodbye.

There is something small and hard nagging at me. Where was the interminable optimism? I recall the few times I had moved from one job to another—less than 10 in my almost 50 years. I had been confident, though, in moving into something even more exciting. I had been excited by the unknown.

I wondered if I was simply older—not just chronologically, but in spirit—in my expectations in life. Had these eight years been successful in transforming me from an eternal optimist to someone who has seen it all? I didn't believe so. I was simply going through a natural transformation, experiencing the temporary White House side effects that comes with working too close to power.

By this time tomorrow, I would no longer be a White House employee. I would have no need for a White House badge, a White House ID number, a White House mess ticket number, a secret code for the Oval Office or a White House pager number.

No one would call and ask if the rumors about the goings-on in the White House were true, or ask where the president and first lady would be vacationing, or whether Vernon Jordan attended the state dinner, or if Princess Di was as tall and skinny in person as she looked on television.

Tomorrow, I would be Janis Q. Public again. I welcomed that return to reality . . . and I dreaded it. A handful of us would continue with the president in his transition office—a six-month stint that would serve as a buffer for him and us. Unlike the hundreds of other White House staffers, we were given time to catch our breaths before stepping both feet out into the real world.

The rude clock on the wall continues its loud ticking, reminding me that my time is fast approaching. It is 10:33 a.m. My husband, Bob, sits at his own desk in the Old Building. I imagine he's having just as hard a time as I am.

The Journey (January 20, 2001)

It was eerie driving through the northwest gate this morning, just as we'd done five or six days a week for five-plus years. The guards recognized us and offered small talk as the drug dogs sniffed our vehicle. The tall, young guard's smile seemed kinder, brighter. He surely knew this was our last day driving through the White House gates.

"You guys have a good life," he said softly, patting Bob's door gently. "We'll miss seeing you come through every day."

We smiled and thanked him for that nice gesture. I am sure one of the reasons they always recognized us was that we were one of the handful of married couples working at the White House.

When Bob and I had married in December 1994, we'd both been working outside the White House. He was undersecretary at the Department of Agriculture, and I was communications director at the Small Business Administration. "Who has time to marry?" I'd complained. But we'd made the time, planning and executing the marriage ceremony in less than six months.

For the last six years of the Clinton administration, Bob was director of presidential personnel, a job that three appointees before him had abandoned. "It's one of those thankless jobs that make you lots of enemies and few friends," was the advice he had received. His long-time loyalty to the president, however, cemented the fact that he'd stay the duration.

Early on, the question of what my job as presidential diarist entailed would come up over dinner, drinks or during other social settings. "How did you end up with such a plum job?" strangers would ask me. After my grand jury experience, however, the questions were flavored with a bit of irony. "A great job, but it must have been hell!"

A job like mine piqued both the public's and the press's curiosity; and to duck the issue, I often joked that I was the official "fly on the White House wall."

It was both humorous and telling when a big name came through the Oval Office to meet the president and they ran into this middle-aged black woman with shoulder length braids walking through the Oval Office or sitting in the back of their meetings quietly taking notes. In the entire five years, there were very few blatant gawkers.

I make a final check of my now-empty desk and signal to the young man that he is free to swipe my computer. I have boxed everything I need and scrapped the rest. The folks coming after me could do whatever their hearts desire with the computer. I push my box to the back corner of my desk before heading down the West Wing hall toward the Oval Office.

I slow my pace, experiencing the strange, ghostly loneliness that has settled into the halls. Even during the few nights I worked past midnight or the times I arrived before daybreak, there was an aliveness to this place. That vigor, though, brought here by the Clintons and their staff had slowly begun its decline some weeks ago. The Bush entourage, I expected, would generate its own flavor of energy.

Today, I witness a West Wing I rarely saw during the Clinton presidency—no meetings, no hurrying to get changes made in the president's speeches, no policy wonks walking the halls ranting or swearing about changes in their scheduled meeting with the president, no visitors peeking in offices to see some recognizable name, no young aides jostling to get the eye or the ear of the president.

I arrive at the outer Oval Office—Betty Currie's domain. I stand at the doorway as the woman who served as President Clinton's personal secretary for the entire eight years finishes up one of her final phone calls as personal secretary to the president.

I am remembering the many mornings I stood in this very spot, chatting with Betty about the day, the president's schedule, sometimes even about our personal lives.

Nancy Hernreich, director of Oval Office operations, sometimes joined us before the president's arrival . . . before the rest of the West Wing came fully to life.

I walk into the Cabinet room, listening with one ear to hear when Betty's conversation ends. The long, stately room took my breath away the first time I stepped inside eight years ago.

The heavy, leather chairs had all been assigned to the important men and women the president chose to lead the federal government. I remember the meetings I sat in on; the repressed volatility of some of the Cabinet meetings. The passion flying about one issue or another . . . faces turning colors, voices rising. The power in those rooms had been heady, indeed, for someone who grew up in the middle of cotton fields.

I had seen power on a much smaller scale back in Arkansas. But only in movies had I seen the awesome power I'd witnessed here in this room, within these walls.

Senators, members of Congress, and other leaders with well-modulated voices, well-coiffed hair, power suits, or dresses. They came in all shapes, sizes and even colors. None of them was infallible, but they were our choices as our lawmakers and decision makers, burdened with the life or death decisions affecting everyday people's lives.

So many of the issues these men and women grappled with had affected my own family and the families of people I'd known and loved—healthcare; welfare reform; the Family Leave Act; the new crime laws, including the hate crime laws; and the infamous Race Initiative. So much power lay in these very human hands.

While I could now easily put a face to the empty chairs, in just weeks the new president would hold his first Cabinet meeting, and those faces would be different. The men and women I'd come to recognize and know would be living their own private lives again. There would be new faces making important decisions about everyday Americans' lives. Quicker than the wink of an eye, the center of power had changed.

I slide my hand along the reflective wood table and the tall chairs as I leave the room. I smile, thinking back to last night and our informal "celebration" of departure from this august place. Twenty or 30 people trickled in and out of Betty's office, toasting our goodbyes, hugging, kissing, tearing up, taking photos for posterity.

As the hour grew late, and the cups of wine caught up with our run-away emotions, Betty and I and a few others had converged in the Cabinet room. We spent much of the next hour remembering together what none of us would ever be able to forget. Before the night became maudlin, Betty remembered a few last minute tasks she needed to attend to—giving the rest of us an excuse to say our goodnights.

I walk back into the sitting area and find Betty and Nancy talking quietly. The anxiety of this morning is left unspoken, but is heavy in the air. We are all anxious for this morning to be over, to say our last goodbyes to the president and each other and begin to pick up the pieces of our real lives.

"Hey." There is a hint of sadness in Betty's smile.

Nancy leans on the door of her small office and offers a sad, tired hello.

"He's late ..." she says, shaking her head, slowly.

We laugh, quietly. Those two words were as old as the man's political career. How many times had Nancy uttered those words in the eight years of Bill Clinton's presidency? But today was the last day of his political career, and that thought cut our laughter short.

"He needs to get over here and do the letter before time for the ceremony in the mansion," Nancy says with a more worried look now. She walks over and peeks through the glass door, then returns to her desk. How many times had she walked across this room and peeked through that door as she checked her watch?

"Betty, do we have the final list for the farewell event?"

Betty searches through piles of documents on her desk and pulls out a single, wrinkled sheet of paper.

"Well, I can tell he's looked at it," she says, "but I don't think he's finished it. There're some names scratched off and some names added . . . and a few question marks."

Nancy smiles and shakes her head. She growls humorously. "Well, who said today should be any different from every other day during the last eight years?"

President William Jefferson Clinton rushes through the glass door that Nancy checked just minutes ago. He is wearing a charcoal gray suit on this last morning of his presidency. He hurries past Betty's desk and Nancy's office.

Buddy, the president's beautiful, chocolate brown Labrador retriever follows him. The president's quick, long strides indicate he knows he is running late, again. He doesn't stop to offer his usual, cheerful, "Good morning, ladies!"

John Podesta, thin and always impeccably dressed, wears a dark suit. He follows closely behind our president of one more day. The intensity of John—always an intense man—is palpable. As chief of staff to a president who is as chronically late as he is brilliant, for John, there is always so much to do and so little time to do it.

The president stands at his desk, reading as if he has the rest of the day to dawdle. Suddenly, he turns and looks through the door at the trio of women. There is the smile that was missing earlier.

"Hey, good morning, ladies!"

We look at each other, smile and respond in unison, "Good morning, Mr. President."

Nancy breathes a sigh of relief as she pulls the Oval Office door closed. She stands for a moment, monitoring his work through the crack in the door. She peeks nervously at her watch. "He's gotta be back over there to greet . . . the new president in 15 minutes."

How many times over the last century had Nancy Hernreich's pressure escalated as she nudged Bill Clinton, the governor, then Bill Clinton, the president, to be where he was supposed to be, on time? She returns to her desk, resumes packing the boxes surrounding it. Worry, though, is written across her thin face. She is hoping things go smoothly and on time this morning. Things somehow usually fall into place in spite of and maybe because of her worry.

John walks through the Oval Office door, stopping long enough to warn Nancy to keep "him" on task.

"He's working on it . . . I'll be back."

The thin, dark man scampers quickly out the door, then down the hall toward the office that won't be his at 12:01 p.m. today.

The president's photographer, Sharon Farmer, rushes, as she sometimes does, through the door. She is toting huge camera equipment on her shoulders and carrying some in her hands.

Sharon looks over at Betty for an OK to go into the Oval Office. This is the last day of the Clinton presidency, and the photos are important for posterity. Betty nods, and Sharon hurries through the Oval Office door. On her heels is a pre-approved former New York Times photographer, who is also cleared to document this last day of the Clinton presidency.

Without speaking, the three of us follow, walking through the door of the Oval Office. We stand quietly against the far wall, watching the informal photo shoot.

This moment and much of this morning seem to move in slow motion. The president looks up and gives the photographer and his aides a weak smile, then resumes his ferocious attempts to complete his task.

He pens the infamous "passing of the presidency" letter on a clean sheet of paper that only has William Jefferson Clinton at the top. He shreds page after page of the unfinished letter. It is a tradition he is upholding: departing presidents leave some words of congratulations, good luck or words of wisdom for the incoming president. Presidents before him had made the notes light and brief. This president seems to be having trouble saying what he has to say in a brief, light way.

"Dear George . . ." one letter begins.

"Dear President Bush," begins another.

"Mr. President," is a third attempt that is quickly tossed into his wastebasket.

At 11 a.m., Doug Band, the president's personal aide, places the brief, but final letter carefully into a small envelope.

President Clinton scribbles across the envelope, then Doug places it in the center of the empty desk, looks at his watch and moves toward the door—a signal to the president to exit.

The president inhales, pulling in a large amount of air, bites his bottom lip, pats his side pockets and turns to look out the Oval Office window. His hands are busy where they are pushed inside his jacket pockets. This is the last time he will stand in the Oval Office or gaze upon the Rose Garden as president of the United States of America.

The Journey (January 20, 2001)

Except for the president standing at the window as he has done so many times before, little else about the almost bare Oval Office is familiar. The warmth and humanity this president brought with him have magically disappeared. The personal effects are gone.

Eight years of memories—gifts from friends and admirers from every corner of the world; the photographs of Hillary and Chelsea, Buddy the dog and Buddy the favorite uncle—are packed away. A photo of the late Commerce Secretary Ron Brown no longer graces the lamp table near the fireplace. It won't be there to remind the next president of the "lows" of the U.S. presidency.

Gone also is the famous Clinton frog collection that had come from across the globe and every corner of the United States. Friends and associates had learned early in his presidency of Bill Clinton's affinity for frogs. They'd sent the president some of the most exquisite, unique, beautiful, humorous frogs in existence. They were great conversation pieces, and this 42nd president never received a frog he didn't love.

Missing, too, is the moon rock that sat on his coffee table and the hundreds of first edition books that kept him company—more gifts from those who knew his unquenchable hunger for words.

The busts of his favorite presidents—Truman, Lincoln, Kennedy and Roosevelt—are also out of sight. The African artifacts, the drum and canes he'd purchased and brought back from his historical Africa trip, are all on their way to the National Archives and Records Administration.

Bill Clinton, just minutes away from mere citizenship, stands with his back to the small group of aides, his hands now clasped behind him. The silence wraps around us. His three Oval Office aides, along with Sharon Farmer, the Times photographer, John Podesta, and Doug Band, all stand motionless, respecting this moment of heart-wrenching silence.

The president turns to face us and offers a weak smile as he moves toward the door, beckoning his staff to him for a final goodbye hug. One by one we hug him as the photographers click away. Tears stream down our cheeks, and we exchange sad smiles.

"I love you . . . I'll miss you," the president says to each of us.

"Take care of Socks," he jokes with Betty, who is now the proud owner and caretaker of the White House cat. ". . . and thanks for everything."

The president smiles as he walks away. He offers a brief salute before going through the door. The photographers and John Podesta follow solemnly and silently. It is also their last morning in the Clinton White House.

I stand now for a while longer with the women in the office before offering my final goodbyes. There is much too much to say and not the time to say it. We hug and wipe tears from our eyes. None of our lives will ever be the same. There will never be another eight years like these.

───⁕───

As I ride with my husband out of the northwest gate, I try for words but none present themselves. The White House guards, recognizing the blue SUV, wave goodbye.

"Good luck, and come back to see us!"

The Journey (January 20, 2001)

How many former White House aides had they offered this kindness to before us? We drive through the gate and ride silently down Pennsylvania Avenue, not looking back.

I close my eyes to the gray, cloudy day and will the door to the last eight years to swing shut. Before beginning the next chapter of my life, I would retrace this amazing journey that delivered me to 1600 Pennsylvania Avenue.

As the White House disappears from the rearview mirror, I am remembering how as a child I'd stared so often out of Mama's kitchen window. While I saw nothing except the endless fields of white cotton, I imagined a world beyond . . . beyond what I'd seen and known on Varner Road. I'd found that world and lived in it for eight memorable years. That world was now behind me, but it would color the rest of my life.

INTERVIEW

Q&A Session with Janis F. Kearney

Q: Your first memoir, *Cotton Field of Dreams,* was centered around your coming of age in the pre-civil rights South. And, though your childhood mirrored the lives of other black families during that time, few black youths today—whether they reside in the South or other parts of the country—can identify with such an existence of dire poverty. Your new memoir, *Something to Write Home About,* also strains believability for most black Americans, as you write about your role serving as a diarist to the president of the United States. What is the correlating thread between these two stories and these two levels of existence?

A: You are so right. *Cotton Field of Dreams* and this second memoir do represent two extreme opposites of existence. On one hand, my environment was poverty and need; and on the other, I was surrounded by power. Yet, in fact, they both proved one truism—the American dream is alive and well.

I am saddened to know so many young people no longer believe there is such a thing available to them. I'm always hopeful, though, that many of them will realize that no one person or group of people have claim to the American dream. It's up for grabs to any of us willing to go for it. It doesn't matter if you're dreaming about making it to the end of the week with a few dollars in your pocket or fantasizing about one day working for the president of the United States. My life stories prove this is as true today as it was a hundred years ago.

Q: On January 20, 2001, you and hundreds of others left the White House, as a new president and his aides took over. You had served in the administration for the entire eight years—five of those years in the White House as personal diarist to the president. What was it like to step outside that kind of experience, back into the "real" world?

A: It was such an amazing eight years for us. Then came the end of it. First, none of us expected to be turning over the White House to the new president, and I think that was the first shocker. But then came the actual walking out of that bubble.

What an unexpected experience, those six or eight months after the White House. I think most of us were hoping we could just close the door to our offices or cubicles, turn in our blue badges, say goodbye to those civil servants who would stay behind, and not ever really have to think about the experience again, unless we chose to.

The opposite is what actually happens. Working in the White House or for a president . . . for most of the people I worked with, changes your life for that time in big and small ways. It is almost true that you breathe a different air. That position is the reason you get up each morning. It's what keeps your adrenaline pumping. And, even though we all thought we were prepared—had actually started preparing months earlier—January 20th was still a surprise.

It was as if our lives came to an abrupt halt. On January 21, we were suddenly at a very strange, awkward, almost painful juncture in our lives, knowing we had to move forward—but not really having the inertia to do so. We hadn't realized how much of our *everything* we'd devoted to that place and time.

It absolutely takes most people six months to get the experience out of their system, to move forward, to get on with their lives—realigning themselves with people and places that were a part of their lives before the White House experience.

Q: What was the greatest challenge for you, as a woman and a minority who worked in the White House and for the Clinton administration? What advice would you give young women who are drawn to politics or government?

A: I wish I could tell you something concrete such as blatant racism or sexism . . . those things we all know still exist, but I can honestly say I wasn't aware of it on a day-to-day basis. My challenges were more personal, like being able to maintain who I was in the midst of what I found myself in. I don't mean the negative things that came and went, but the side effects of that aphrodisiac-like allure of power and prestige—things that can taint your integrity, your sense of who you really are . . . if you're not careful.

As I said earlier, it is actually a little like breathing a different air. Even when you may not believe there is anything special about who you are, others are convinced there must be and begin to treat you that way. So, simply keeping my head and making sure my feet stayed on solid ground . . . that was my challenge. So was remembering from whence I came and how many people had sacrificed so that I could sit where I sat each day. My challenge also was to constantly remind myself that I wasn't there because I was so special, or smart or indispensable.

What would I advise young women seeking roles in politics or government? I'd say Hurrah! Go for it, and never let anyone tell you that you can't or shouldn't pursue your goal. What America needs is more good politicians and a more diverse array of good politicians. Women have to be committed. We have to be willing to learn and willing to work very, very hard. With those values in place, there is no reason we can't do or be whatever it is we desire to be.

Q: Why did you take seven years to write this second installment of your memoir?

A: Actually, I began working on this book immediately after I left the White House. It just turned out that I had two other stories already in the hopper that needed to be told first.

As publisher of a small press, in addition to being the primary author, I find myself making decisions constantly as to which stories have to be told, and when. It's as if I'm placing them on a mental assembly line and plucking them off only when that little voice tells me their time has come.

I must say, there are lots of reasons I believe this story is important now—in the midst of so much dismal news and hopelessness. I pray that my story touches young people, that those interested in politics find some redemption here, come away knowing that there is so much good "mere" politicians can do if only they will.

Q: You compare your time in the White House to *Alice in Wonderland*. In the story Alice follows a "mysterious white rabbit" into a mysterious world "populated by peculiar creatures." Was there a mystic in President Clinton that was different from that of Governor Clinton? Also, was there something that stood out in your mind (good or bad) that was especially "peculiar" about the Clinton administration?

A: I compare it to *Alice in Wonderland* in two different contexts. But the white rabbit is really my challenge to my sense of discovery, exploration—of getting outside my 30 plus-year comfort zone.

Leaving Arkansas and moving to a place like D.C. was a major, major cultural leap. Here I was in my late 30s, finding myself in a whole new world—having to learn the complex "take no enemies" political culture that would now be my life 24-7. So, that was the Alice in me, at one level.

Then, at another level, the change was more of an intrinsic upheaval. The "me" I'd always been was being forced to change to some extent, simply for survival. I was fighting hard to hold onto the lessons and the values I'd always held onto. I knew I would have to get up each day and do the things I was brought to D.C. to do, and accept that nothing would be as it had been in the past—the experiences, the level of friendships and family I was accustomed to. None of that was here. As Alice likely was, I was afraid, and early on, often sad. But, at the same time, there was an undeniable excitement about this change. I was challenged. And I bet there isn't much difference in me and Alice in how we love challenges.

Q: How would you describe that magical bridge that took you from Varner Road to 1600 Pennsylvania Avenue? Is that a bridge that other blacks and women have access to . . . no matter where they begin their journey?

A: Yes, yes, that same bridge I crossed can be crossed from any point in the universe, by anyone willing to cross it. It doesn't matter *where* you begin, but it does matter who you begin your journey with; what takes place during those earliest years in your starting place.

It doesn't matter if you start out in the cotton fields, or in the Appalachian mountains, or on an Indian reservation, or right on the other side of the Mexican border . . . the bridge is permanent, sitting there waiting for you. Dreams, hopes, hard work, and, yes, prayer are the things that will help you cross that bridge. There's really nothing magic about any of that.

Q: In reading *Cotton Field of Dreams*, we know there were so many invaluable lessons from Varner Road that you took along with you throughout your journey. But what are some lessons you learned and took with you when you left the White House in 2001?

A: The greatest lesson was an appreciation and better understanding of politics. Here was something I'd never held much appreciation for, even though I'd grown up listening to my father talk about politics constantly. He loved politics and had an innate understanding of it. But the part of politics he shared with us was more of the negatives about how it was used against so many people. I understood that, and I formulated my disdain for politics based on that.

So, as a young adult, I had no real respect for politicians. I laid most of this country's ills at the feet of the politicians I considered either weak or dishonest. The opportunity to see firsthand that there actually is a thing I now describe as good politics was a wonderful evolution, especially to be able to share with my dad what *good* politics was doing for everyday people like us. That was a great and important lesson for me.

The second most important lesson was not a new one. But working inside the White House bubble gave me a good opportunity to relearn it: Every man puts on his pants one leg at a time. Simply put, we're born, we live, we die. No one, no matter how smart, how beautiful, how rich, how powerful does it any other way. So, how in the world does one person get to call himself or herself greater than someone else . . . based on what?

I often say the greatest lesson I learned in going to an integrated school was the powerful lesson that white skin didn't make others smarter or harder working, or nicer. Working at the White House taught me that power doesn't make a person great. We're all human beings, blessed or cursed with different opportunities, and even how we choose to use those opportunities doesn't raise us up beyond being simply human.

INDEX

Boldface indicates photographs.

A
Abernathy, Donzaleigh, **275**
Abernathy, Ralph, 275
Adams, Ashley, **263**
Advocacy journalism, 38
Agassi, Andre, **275**, 286
Alfred, Lord Tennyson, 201
Alice in Wonderland, comparison of time in White House to, 307–308
Allen, James, **277**
AmeriCorps, 210
Anderson, David, 142, 151
Andrews, Julie, **275**, 286
Angelou, Maya, 129–130, 135
Arkansas
    Christmas in, 194
    homeless in, 174
    school killing in, 244
Arkansas Democrat Gazette, stories on Lewinsky scandal, 233–235
Arkansas State Press
    advertising in, 46
    advocacy journalism at, 38
    anniversary celebration of, 155, 160–163
    Bates, Daisy as consultant at, 47–48
    Bates, Daisy decision to retire from, 41–42
    changes in, 39, 44–45
    co-founding of, 37–38
    commitment to community, 39
    day-to-day operations of, 45–46
    early days at, 37
    employees of, 48
    financial standings of, 46
    interview for managing editor position at, 34–35
    Janis, as managing editor, 35, 40–41
    Janis' decision to purchase, 42–48
    move of offices, 48
    presidential campaign coverage by, 49–50
    revival of, 38
    shadowing of Don (managing editor) at, 36
    stories reported by, 38
Arlington, Ohio, 21st Century Express stop in, 209
Ashland, Kentucky, 21st Century Express stop in, 209

B

Bacon Memorial District Library, 210
Band, Doug, 242, 296, 298
Barnes, Beverly, **267**
Bates, Daisy Gatson, 25, **261**
   at anniversary celebration of *Arkansas State Press*, 163–164
   as civil rights legend, 31
   co-founding of *Arkansas State Press* by, 37–38
   continued work as consultant at newspaper, 47–48
   decision to retire from newspaper, 41–42
   health problems of, 38, 39, 42
   Janis and, 45, 214, **261**
   loss of *Arkansas State Press*, 37–38
   at Mitchelville Economic Opportunity Agency, 31, 39
   need for managing editor at newspaper, 31, 34–35
   personality of, 37
   revival of *Arkansas State Press*, 38
   speech impairment of, 35
   strokes of, 35
   work of, with Democratic National Committee, 31
Bates, L. C., 37
   co-founding of *Arkansas State Press* by, 37–38
   death of, 38
   Janis' admiration of, 45
   loss of *Arkansas State Press*, 37–38
Bates Scholarship Committee, **261**
Battle Creek, Michigan, 21st Century Express stop in, 210, 214

Birmingham church bombings, 244
Black newspapers
   advertising for, 46–47
   community and, 46–47
Blythe, Billy, 210
Bono, **271**, 286
Bowles, Erskine, 189, **267**
   move to deputy chief of staff to president, 181
   at Small Business Administration, 180–181, 188
Breuer, Lannie, 231
Broren, Katie, 147
Brown, Alma, 200, 201
Brown, Alvin, 147
Brown, Michael, 201
Brown, Patrice, 115, 162
Brown, Ron, 248, 250, 297
   Clinton's eulogy for, 201
   crash of plane in Croatia, 198–200
   death of, 201–202
   funeral of, 201–201
Browne, Harry, 217
*Bryan (press office intern), 65
Buchanan, Pat, 188
Buddy (Lavrador retriever), 244, 294, 297
Bumpers, Dale, 19 20
Bush, George H. W., administration of, 73
Bush, George W., 282

C

Cabe, Gloria, **269**
Calloway family, 11
Cameron, Rebecca, 188
Carpenter, Liz, 196
Carter, Jimmy, administration, presidential diarist position in, 184, 190

Carville, James, 49
Cherry blossom season, 179
Chicago, 21st Century Express arrival in, 211–212
Chillicothe, Ohio, 21st Century Express stop in, 209
Christmas
  in Arkansas, 194
  memories of Varner Road at, 190–191
  in Washington, D.C., 179, 190, 192–194
Civil rights
  Clinton and, 202–205, 245–247, 292
  Johnson and, 204
  Kennedy and, 204
Clay, Eartha, 210–211
Clinton, Chelsea
  on election night 1992, 59–60
  at first inauguration, 128
  1996 reelection campaign and, 210, 217, 218
Clinton, Hillary Rodham, 146
  celebration of Christmas in White House and, 193–194
  early meeting with Janis, 72
  on election night 1992, 59–60
  at first inauguration, 128
  holiday vacations of, 195
  with Janis, **267**
  as law professor, 52, 71, xv
  1996 reelection campaign and, 207, 210, 211, 216
  Yale law degree of, 71
Clinton, William Jefferson, **265, 267**
  ability to compartmentalize, 228
  African tour of, 244
  AmeriCorps program of, 210
  as Arkansas attorney general, 19, 72
  as astute politician, 223–224
  Brown, Ron, and, 200, 201
  Buddy and, 244
  cabinet of, 224
  celebration of Christmas in White House and, 193–194
  charisma of, 72–73
  civil rights and, 202–205
  description of, 224–226
  early meeting with Janis, 50, 72
  on election night 1992, 59–60
  election of, as governor, 20
  eulogy for Brown, Ron, 201
  eulogy for Jordan, Barbara, 195–196
  at first Inauguration, 123–130
  first presidential campaign of, 49–50, 52–53
  frog collection of, 297
  fundraising by, 206
  as governor, 19, 52, 70, 72
  holiday vacations of, 195
  with Janis, **265**
  last day in office, 293–298
  as law professor, 52, 71, xv
  leadership of, 239–240
  left of center common sense approach of, 73
  legacy of, 146, 244
  letters to, 229
  Lewinsky sex scandal and, 226
  1996 reelection and, 206–212
  as not a micromanager, 243
  One America Race Initiative and, 202–205, 245–247, 292
  presentation of award to Bates, Daisy, **261**
  public appearances of, 224
  reelection and, 216–219
  Republican-led Congress and, 223

313

resiliency of, 223
speech to the Convocation of the Church of God, 229–230
tagging of staff as blind loyalists to, 239–240
third State of the Union Address of, 196–197
trip to Chicago convention on 21st Century Express, 206–212
trip to St. Petersburg, Russia, 242
use of politics by, xiii
voice of, xii
welfare reform policy of, 214–215
Yale law degree of, 71
young people in White House of, 68
Coca-Cola summer enrichment programs, 57
Cogdell, Patti, **263**
Coleman, Justin, **269**
Colorado school killing, 244
Columbus, Ohio, 21st Century Express stop in, 209
"Contract with America," 223
Cotton Field of Dreams, 303, 308–309
Craig, Greg, 231
Crime, in Washington, D.C., 180
Cummins Prison, 3, 96
Currie, Betty, 187, 198–199, **265**, **267**, **269**, 291, 292–293, 294
  Socks and, 298
Cyrus, Billy Ray, 209

D

Daley, Richard M., 52–53
Dallek, Bob, 185
Davis, Lannie, 231

preparation of Janis for Grand Jury testimony, 232–233
Democratic National Convention, 50–51
De Niro, Robert, 286
Dixieville, New Hampshire, 217
Dole, Bob, 206, 217, 218
Dora Bell Church, 15

E

Education
  Freedom of Choice in, 21
  segregated, 21
Eisenhower, Mamie, 245, 247, 269
Eldridge, James, 210
Eller, Jeff
  as communications guru, 69–70
  as White House media affairs director, 69–70, 73–74, 78–79, 131, 141–142, 150–151
Engskov, Kris, 242, **265**
"ER," cast members from, 286

F

Family Leave Act, 291
Farmer, Sharon, **277**, 295, 298
Faubus, Orval, 18–19
Fawcette, John, 183, 184, 185
Fillmore, Charlotte, 245–247, **269**
  death of, 247
  invitation to White House, 245–247
  one hundredth birthday of, 245, 247
First Baptist Church, 15, 90–91
Fisher, George, 201
Flipper, Henry O., 244
Frances (migrant child), 15–16

Freedom of Choice, 21

G
Gatlin, Patsy, 31–32, 34
Georgetown University, 171–172
Gingrich, Newt, 223
Glenn, John, 209, 214
Goldberg, Whoopi, **273**, 286
Goodin, Stephen, 188, 242
Goodwin, Doris Kearns, 185
Gore, Al, 51, 216
Gorée Island, Clinton visit to, 244
Gould, Arkansas, 15, 27
   life in, 14
   politics in, 20–21
   poverty in, 22–23
   town leaders in, 25
Grady, Arkansas, 15, 158
Grapevine (campus newspaper), 33
Great Migration, 9–10, 14

H
Harding, Warren G., xv
Harris, E. Lynn, 57
Hate crimes, 256
Henderson, Mary, 96
Herman, Alexis, 200, 201
Hernreich, Nancy, **267, 269**
   on presidential diarist position, 184–185, 226–227, 231
   21st Century Express Tour of middle America and, 207
   as White House Oval Office director, 182–187, 198, 207, 284, 291, 293, 294–295
   work of, in governor's office, 187

Hill, Dule, **275**
Homeless
   in Arkansas, 174
   in Washington, D.C., 174–175, 180
Hope, Arkansas, 223
Howard University Choir, 201
Huntington, 21st Century Express departure from, 208

J
Jackson, Mary, 96
Jackson, Nola Mae, 8
Jackson, Robert, 8
Jackson, Verline, 96
Jefferson, Thomas, xiv
Jim Crow era, 22
Joel, Billy, **271**
Johnson, Alma, 112, 114–117
Johnson, Ben, 245, 246
Johnson, Jim, 19
Johnson, Lyndon B., 210
   administration of, 31, 164
   blame of, for Vietnam War, 17–18
   civil rights under, 204
   hiring of individual to chronicle presidency of, 185
   inauguration of, 128
   Kearney, James on, 17–18
   Territo as special assistant to, 183
Johnson, Robert, 201
Jones Day (law firm), 250
Jordan, Barbara
   Clinton's eulogy for, 195–196
   death of, 195
Jordan, Michael, **271**
Jordan, Vernon, 288
Journalism, advocacy, 38

K

Kalamazoo, Michigan, 21st Century Express stop in, 211
Kearney, Brandon (nephew), at Kearney reunion, **259**
Kearney, Ethel Virginia Curry (mother), 3, 7, 8, 82, 89, 132, **259**
   caregiver role of, 101–102, 103
   character of, 6
   children of, 5, 13
   death from cancer, 86, 97–98
   heroes of, 25
   lessons learned from, ix–x, xvii
   marriage of, 13
Kearney, James (father), 3, 7, 8–9, 10, 97–111
   aging of, 281, 285
   agriculture extension agent and, 24
   at anniversary celebration of *Arkansas State Press*, 163–164
   baptism of Janis and, 93, 94–95
   bond with Janis, 86–87, 97–102
   brush with presidency, xv–xvi
   character of, 6
   children of, 5, 13
   as dreamer, 6
   heroes of, 25
   Janis' decision to go to Washington and, 84–85, 104–111
   Janis' promise to visit, 143
   at Kearney reunion, 167–168, **259**
   lessons learned from, 26–27, 256, ix–x, xvii
   letters from Janis to, 121–122, 134–135, 165–166, 213–215
   marriage of, 13
   on need for black participation in change, 20, 21
   on need for welfare, 23–25
   on politics, 16–23, 24, 51
   on poll taxes, 25
   as sharecropper, 11–12, 13
   as Sunday School Superintendent at Rankin Chapel Church, 10
   visiting, 158–161
   voting and, 24–25
Kearney, Janetta (sister), 70, 75–86, 100, 161, 162
   business travel to Hawaii, 111–112
   early years of, 77
   education of, 81–82
   at Hughes Aircraft Company, 82
   at Kearney reunion, **259**
   at newspaper, 155
Kearney, Janeva (sister), at Kearney reunion, **259**
Kearney, Janis Faye, **263**
   with Abernathy, Donzaleigh, **275**
   admiration of, for the Bates, 45
   on African safari, **269**
   with Agassi, Andre, **275**
   with Allen, James, **277**
   with Andrews, Julie, **275**
   at anniversary celebration of *Arkansas State Press*, 155, 160–163
   automobile ownership and, 172, 173
   baptism of, 91–96
   Bates, Daisy, desire to retire and, 41–42
   with Bates, Daisy, **261**

Index

beggers and, 173–175
birth of son, 33
bond with father, 86–87, 97–102
with Bono, **271**
as caregiver for father, 97–111
as CETA project assistant director, 72
childhood on Varner Road, 3–27, 190–191
Clinton, William and, 144–145, **265**
with Clinton, Hillary, **267**
in Clinton-Gore 1996 campaign press office, 52–53, 60–61
in Clinton-Gore transition office's press department, 61, 65
Clinton inauguration and, 123–130
college life of, 32–33, 132
as communications manager at the Small Business Administration, 151–152
commute to work by, 172–173
comparison of time in White House to *Alice in Wonderland*, 307–308
coverage of Democratic National Convention by, 50–51
creative writing by, 33
with D. K., **259**
dating of Nash, Bob, 55
death of sister, Jo Ann, 31, 36–37
decision of son, to go to Morehouse College, 48
decision on offering of position in White House Office of Media Affairs, 74, 78–87
decision to leave White House, 150–151
decision to marry Nash, Bob, 168–169
decision to purchase *Arkansas State Press*, 42–48
on description of Clinton, William, 224–226
as director of information at Migrant Data Bank, 32, 36
with D.K. and daughter-in-law, Pamela, **269**
early job opportunity with Bates, Daisy, 31
early meeting with Clinton, 50
education of, 26–27
efforts to visit Arkansas, 143
on election night 1992, 59–60
Eller, Jeff and, 69–70
explaining of decision to go to Washington to father, 84–85
with Farmer, Sharon, **277**
FBI clearance of, 126, 186
first marriage of, 33
freelancing for *Grapevine* (campus newspaper), 33
friendship with Bates, Daisy, 45, 214, **261**
with Goldberg, Whoopi, **273**
as government worker, 33
graduation photo of, **259**
with Hill, Dule, **275**
honeymoon with Nash, 170
interview for presidential diarist position, 182–183
interview with Bates, 34–35
interview with Small Business Administration, 147–149
job at Lincoln County courthouse, 31
with Joel, Billy, **271**

with Jordan, Michael, **271**
jury duty of, 197–198
at Kearney reunion, 167–168, **259, 269**
with King, B.B., **275**
knowledge of governors, 18–19
leaving of White House by, 248, 281–299, 304–305
letters to father, 121–122, 134–135, 165–166, 213–215
life in Washington, 132–133, 136–175, 240–241, 243
living with Nash, Bob, 136, 137–138, 139, 140, 143, 144, 165–166
as managing editor at *Arkansas State Press*, 40–41
marriage to Nash, 169, 289
at Media Affairs Office, 144
memoirs of, 303
move to Little Rock, 33
move to Washington, 111, 112–113
naivety of, on politics, 67
Nash, Bob and, 74, 136, 137–138, 139, 140, 143, 144, 150, 154, 165–166
offering of job as managing editor, 35
offering of position at Small Business Administration, 150
with Parks, Rosa, **273**
with Poitier, Sidney, **273**
police racism and, 250–256
as political cynic, 51
preparation for Grand Jury testimony, 232–233
as presidential diarist, 180–181, 186–190, 225, 231, 234, 289–290
rediscovery of normalcy by, 240, 243
religious conversion of, 87–91
sabbatical from newspaper, 65
shadowing of Don (managing editor) at *Arkansas State Press*, 36
with Sheen, Martin, **273**
siblings of, 5, 12–13
at Small Business Administration, 170
with Smith, Will and Jana Pinkett, **271**
subpoena for, during Starr investigation, 227
transport of D. K. to Morehouse College and, 55–58
on 21st Century Express tour, 206–212, **265**
Upshur Street house of, 170–172
use of wedding planner, 169
visit to Arkansas, 155–158
visit with father, 158–161
as White House Media Affairs officer, 125–128, 141–144, xvi–xvii
White House salary of, 146, 150–151
with Williams, Serena, **271**
writing as calling of, 32
with Wyclef, **273**
Kearney, Jeffery, at Kearney reunion, **259**
Kearney, Jerome (brother), 101, 109
Kearney, Jesse (brother), 72
as Arkansas assistant attorney general, 72
at Kearney reunion, **259**

318

as liaison to Arkansas Department of Local Services, 72
Kearney, Jo Ann (sister), 87, 96, 102–103
   death of, 31, 36–37, 87
   at Kearney reunion, **259**
   personality of, 37
   religious conversion of, 88
Kearney, John (brother), at Kearney reunion, **259**
Kearney, John-John (nephew), at Kearney reunion, **259**
Kearney, Jude (brother), 101, 167
   Brown, Ron, and, 199
   at Kearney reunion, **259**
   move to Johannesburg, 248–250, 251
   taking of partnership with LeBoef Lamb, 248
Kearney, Jude, Jr. (nephew), move to Johannesburg, 248
Kearney, Julius (brother)
   catering of wedding of Janis and Bob and, 169
   at Kearney reunion, **259**
Kearney, Kathryn (niece), move to Johannesburg, 248
Kearney, Lorraine (sister-in-law), 167, 199
   move to Johannesburg, 248–249
Kearney reunion, 167–168, **259, 269**
Kelly, Virginia, 129
Kennedy, John F., 25, 208, 238, 297, xii
   assassination of, 87
   blame of, for Vietnam War, 17, 18
   civil rights under, 204
   inauguration of, 128
   Kearney, James on, 18
   young people in White House of, 67
Kennedy, Robert, 25
King, B. B., **275**
King, Martin Luther, Jr., 25
   as alumni of Morehouse, 53
King, Rodney, 249, 251, 254
Ku Klux Klan, 19

L

Lader, Phil, 181
   as ambassador to United Kingdom, 181
   annual Renaissance weekend of, 195
Land, Henry, 97
Land, Oldie Lee, 96
Lanier, Bob, 196
Larson, Todd, 72
LaVelle, Avis, 52–53
LeBoef Lamb, 248, 250
Lee, Barbara, 196
Lewinsky, Monica, 235
Lewinsky sex scandal, 226, 231, 233–235
Liberal Democrats, 21
Liberal politicians, 19
Lieberman, Evelyn, **265**
Lincoln, Abraham, 211, 297
   election train tour of, 207
   Kearney, James on, 18
Lincoln County courthouse, Janis at, 31
Lindsey, Bruce, **269**
"The Little Engine That Could," 210
Little Rock, integration of Central High School in, 18–19, 38
Lunon, D. K. (son), 33, 75, 76, 83, 97–98, 156, 166
   childhood of, 54–55
   decision to go to Morehouse College, 48, 53–54

319

friends of, 54
graduation from college, 285
graduation from high school, 53
at high school, 48
on Janis' move to Washington, 112–113
at Kearney reunion, 167
at Moorehead College, 82, 83
with mother, **259**
with mother and wife, **269**
on mother working at White House, 122
newspaper and, 48–49
participation in Coca-Cola summer enrichment program, 57
support from, on purchase of newspaper, 42–43
teenage years of, 40
transport to Morehead College, 55–58
Lunon, Darryl (first husband), 33, 54, 83, 102
gardening by, 76–77
move to Little Rock, 33
support from, on purchase of newspaper, 42–43
Lunon, Pamela (daughter-in-law), with husband and Janis, **269**

M

Manchester, New Hampshire, 216
Mandala, Nelson, 244
Mariano, Connie, 205
Marsalis, Wynton, 201
McCatharan, Ellen, 189–190
McDonald, Anne Marie, ix
Michigan City, Indiana, 21st Century Express stop in, 211
Migrant Data Bank, 32

giving of notice at, 36
Million Man March, 196
Mills, Cheryl, 231
Montgomery County Police, 253
Moose, Charles, 254
Morehouse College (Atlanta)
King as alumni of, 53
son's decision to attend, 48, 53–54
Myers, Dee Dee, 49, 53, 65–68
as White House press secretary, 66

N

Nash, Bob, 133, 143, **263, 269**
on African safari, **269**
at anniversary celebration of *Arkansas State Press*, 162–163
automobile ownership and, 172, 173
beggers and, 173–174
commute to work by, 172–173
dating of Janis, 55
in D.C. transition office, 85–86
as director of Arkansas Finance and Development Agency, 55
as director of presidential personnel at White House, 182, 208, 234, 289
discussion of next phase of life, 282
first marriage of, 169
gardening interests of, 170
honeymoon with Janis, 170
Janis and, 74, 136, 137–138, 139, 140, 143, 144, 150, 154, 165–166
on leaving White House, 248, 288–289

Index

life in Washington, 240–241, 243
loyalty to Clinton, 182
marriage to Janis, 289
police racism and, 250–256
rediscovery of normalcy by, 240, 243
as senior economic aide to Clinton, 55
transport of D. K. to Morehouse College, 55–58
as undersecretary at the U.S. Department of Agriculture, 150, 166, 170
Upshur Street house of, 170–172
visit to Arkansas, 155
in Washington, 123, 136, 137–138, 139–140
work in post administration transition office, 282–283
National Newspaper Publishers Association, 46
Newspaper publishing, challenge of, 43
New Works Program, 210
Nixon, Richard, visit in Ashland, Kentucky, 209
Norman, Jessye, 218

O
Oklahoma bombing, 244
Old Executive Office Building, 130, 284
One America Race Initiative, 202–205, 245–247
"On the Pulse of Morning" (Angelou), 129
Oval Office, 130

P
Pace, Judy, 81
*Pam, 188, 189

Panetta, Leon, 181
Parks, Deacon, 93, 94–95
Parks, Rosa, 209, 214, **273**
Perkins, Danny, 162
Perot, Ross, 217
Pine Bluff, Arkansas, 8–9, 26, 156, 158
Pine Bluff Commercial (newspaper), 25
Podesta, John, 294, 295, 298
Poitier, Sidney, **273**
Police racism, 250–256
Politics, Clinton, Bill's, use of, xiii
Poll taxes, 25
Potomac Fever, 153
Powell, Colin, **263**
Powell, Mrs. Colin, **263**
Presidential diarist, 182–185
hiring of Janis as, 186–190
job of, 225, 226–227, 289–290
Princess Di, 288
Progressive politicians, 21
Pryor, David, 19

R
Rankin Chapel, 10, 15, 90–91, 111
Reagan, Ronald, 238
administration of, 73, 188
Republicans, 19
Richardson, Ann, 196
Rockefeller, Jay, 171
Rockefeller, Winthrop, 19
Roosevelt, Franklin D., 206, 210, 211, 218, 238, 297
inauguration of, 128
Kearney, James on, 18
New Works Program of, 210
Rudolph, B. A., **269**
Ruff, Charles, 231
Rumph, Josephine, 61, 70, 74, 162
Rushman, Nichole, 210

S
Senegal, Clinton visit to, 244
Sharecropping, 11
Sheen, Martin, **273**
Sioux Falls, Dakota, 216
Slater, Rodney, **269**
Small Business Administration
   under Bowles, 180–181, 188
   Janis as communications manager at, 150, 151–152
   Janis' interview with, 147–149
   under Lader, 181
   need for FBI clearance to work for, 126, 186
   upgrading to cabinet-level department, 180
Smith, Arnold, 162
Smith, Jada Pinkett, **271**, 286
Smith, Will, **271**, 286
Socks (presidential cat), 298
Something to Write Home About, 303
   writing of, 306–307
Sosa, Sammy, 286
Southern Delta
   blacks in, 21–22
   poverty in, 22–23
Southern Methodist University, 54
Star City, Arkansas, 23
Starr, Kenneth, 226, 227
State of the Union Addresses, 196–197, xv
Stephanopoulos, George, 49, 187
Strauss, Richard, 151

T
Taft, William H., 210
Territo, Dorothy, 183, 184, 185
The Way the Crow Flies (McDonald), ix
"This Land is Your Land," 216
"This Little Light of Mine," 196
Thomasson, Patsy, **269**
Tio, Maria, 141, 142
Trimble, Don, as managing editor at *Arkansas State Press*, 34–35, 36
Truman, Harry S, 209, 297
Tudjman, Franjo, 200
21st Century Express
   Clinton's tour of middle America on, 206–212, **265**
   passengers on, 208–209

V
Varner Road
   childhood life on, 3–27, 190–191
   churches on, 15
   Cummins Prison on, 3, 96
   families on, 8–10, 14–16
   return visit to, 158–161
Vietnam War, blame for, 17–18

W
Walker, Jerry Jeff, 216
Ward, Nancy, **263**
Washington, C. L. (Reverend), 89–90, 92, 93, 94–95
Washington, D.C.
   cherry blossom season in, 179
   Christmas in, 179, 190, 192–194
   crime in, 180
   homeless in, 174–175, 180
   life in, 179–180, 240–241, 243
   media on, 179
   presidential election season in, 205–206
Washington, George, xiv
   presidency of, 237
Welfare system
   failure of, 23

reform in, 214–215
"West Wing," cast members from, 130, **273, 275, 286**
White House
　Christmas at, 192-194
　media pool for, 241–242
White House Media Affairs office, 130–131, **263**
White House Radio office, 142
White House Television Office, 142
Whitney, Justin, 210
Wilkins family, 8–9
Williams, Maggie, 49
Williams, Serena, **271**, 286
Williams, Venus, 286
Willis, Carol, **263, 269**
Witherspoon, Mary, 106–107
Wyclef, **273**
Wynadotte, Michigan, 21st Century Express stop in, 210

Y

Yellow Dog Democrats, 21, 132

Z

Zahn, Paula, 209

Go to the Writing Our World Press e-book store to order other **Janis F. Kearney** titles: www.writingourworldpress.com

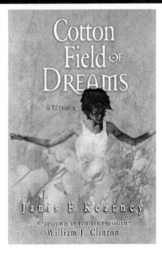

Cotton Field of Dreams: A Memoir/ ISBN: 09762058-0-7/ paperback - $15.95

Conversations: William Jefferson Clinton...From Hope to Harlem/ ISBN: 09762058-1-5/ hardback - $27.95; paperback - $19.95

Once Upon a Time There Was a Girl: A Murder at Mobile Bay/ ISBN: 978-09762058-6-9/ hardback-$22.95

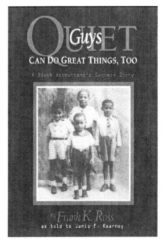

Quiet Guys Can Do Great Things Too: A Black Accountant's Success Story by Frank Ross and Janis F. Kearney/ ISBN: 09762058-3-2 / paperback - $19.95

Become a "Friends of WOW! Books" member, and get a 20% discount immediately, when ordering 10 copies or more.

Printed in the United States
136093LV00002B/22/P